CLEVEDON'S SOCIAL AND INDUSTRIAL HERITAGE

Further studies in the history of Clevedon

Published by the Clevedon Civic Society 1998

Reprinted 2000/02/04

ISBN 1 901 084 17 5

Contents

Foreword

In 1829, when John Rutter produced his guide book to Clevedon, he extolled its picturesque beauty at some length but gave no hint that there was rather more than mild air and delightful walks to recommend it. No doubt he, like the guide book writers that followed, discounted the interest of the long-established weaving industry or the limekilns and quarries and what they contributed to the character of the town.

It is only now, in the late 20th century, that this attitude towards industrial history has begun to change and the impact of technology on town and country explored by enlightened local historians. In their latest publication, the Clevedon Civic Society gives an excellent example of what can and should be done in this field.

Names like Percy Daniel, Binding and Payne or Willcocks will be familiar to many Clevedonians but this book shows us the true scale of their achievments, nationally as well as locally. Shopland is another well-known name but how many of us realised before now that so many of the architectural features which give charm and distinction to Clevedon's streetscape came from their brickworks and sawmills? And in future, as we take those leafy walks so much admired by Rutter, we will be aware that the town owes its public health, clean air and sweet smells to the 19th century engineers who provided it with fresh drinking water,main drainage,gas and electricity, all amenities we take so much for granted today.

The Civic Society is planning a further publication on Clevedon's industrial heritage. This reader, for one, can hardly wait.

Julia Elton

Vice President, Clevedon Civic Society

Introduction

What was the first industry in Clevedon?

Well, in addition to food, keeping warm was important, and no doubt weaving and the associated processes of making clothes came high on the list of priorities. Tucking or fulling mills may have been established as early as 1340 on the river opposite Clevedon Court; they were certainly there in 1630.

Remains of pot making and iron smelting have been found in the surrounding areas, so these seem likely to become contenders for inclusion in the list.

Five old limekilns are still to be seen around the town, so lime burning was a thriving activity which would require the limestone to be quarried first. Building stone would be needed, too, and thatchers would be cutting reed on the moors to roof the houses. Tools would be needed, so the blacksmith would be forging the drills, hammers and chisels for the skilled workmen. There were a number of forges in the town, the oldest being the one sited where the Pharmacy of the Health Centre now stands, in Old Street. It has been traced back to 1660.

In 1680, a permit was obtained to dig for lead on Court Hill, where some of the holes, or grooves, can still be seen. Then in 1689, permission was given to establish salt pans on Salthouse Fields at the sea front. The workers lived in two cottages which were eventually combined to make the present hotel, The Salthouse. They would need wagons to take the salt to market, pulled by horses which would need shoeing, and with iron-rimmed wheels - back to the blacksmith again.

In 1630, there was a coppice of forty years growth on Court Hill; here the charcoal burner comes in, as well the many by products of the coppice - wood for thatching pins for instance.

The charcoal burner was probably the least dependent on tools but as the provider of an efficient source of fuel was likely to have been the catalyst for the start-up of an industrial section of the local community.

Historical records show that at different times there were at least four blacksmiths, seven limekilns, several quarries producing both limestone and sandstone plus the saltpans so although the local population was small until the town began really to grow in the middle of the nineteenth century, they must have been quite busy.

Therefore together with farming and fishing, Clevedon grew up with quite a good economy for a relatively isolated community.

As the population grew so did the range of industries, some still with us, others replaced to match the needs and fashions of the day. Now, with a population approaching 25,000, the tradition set in those far off days continues, and the following pages give some indication of the wide and varied base of trades and industries of which Clevedon is justly proud.

Brickworks and Potteries in Clevedon

I shan't be dealing with any pottery sites from archaeological times, but working my way forward from the middle of the last century. There must have been places locally from where pottery for the home could be procured - notably Ham Green in the fourteenth century, but I have stuck to what I know!

The early industrial potteries were the brickworks. There were two, one run by the Shopland family in Kenn Road, the other a longer-running concern in Strode Road managed by different people at different times.

Strode Road Brickworks

There was a large brickworks just above the junction of Strode Road with Southern Way. They were, I think, the first brickworks in the town, and were run by William Wilcox. He had been in Weston-super-Mare for many years, and seems to have come to Clevedon in the 1860s. Many of the houses in Strode Road were built by him in the years between 1867 and 1869, with patterns built into the brick fronts. Many have been rendered over, unfortunately. Where did the workers come from?

Before men were trained locally, they moved up from the area around Bridgwater, where bricks had been made for generations - on the Somerset Levels, there are no stone quarries! In the 1871 Census, in Strode Road, there are 3 brick and tile makers from Bridgwater, 1 from nearby Combwich, a brickmaker and a pipe maker from Cannington and a potter from Clapham. Another man who may have been working in association with the brickworks was a china and glass moulder from Bristol.

Mr Wilcox retired in 1885, and Conway G Warne took over the management of the brickworks. He also had come from one of the brickworks in Weston-super-Mare, and had been in partnership with Wilcox for 3 years.

The Strode Road Brickworks was only one of their companies, as they had retained the firm called the Original Pottery in Weston-super-Mare, and in 1888, Warne took over the Royal Pottery there as well. There was increasing demand for bricks and tiles, but Warne also patented two products used nationally, a land drain well and an electric cable trough.

In 1894, Sidney Keen took over at Strode Road, having worked as company manager at the Weston site. Like Warne, he was involved with the local Volunteers, in the form of the Royal Engineers First Devon and Somerset Volunteers, who used the rifle range at Tickenham, and is remembered locally as Colonel Keen. Keen's Way is named after him.

The three photographs here show firstly the pottery being demolished, with scaffolding around the kiln chimney, and secondly Sidney Keen's business card - Sidney Keen and Brother, with a view of the old brickworks in their days of glory. The third picture shows the extent of the pits where they dug out the clay, before the flooded area was filled in. Britannia Windows and the sports centre are near the site.

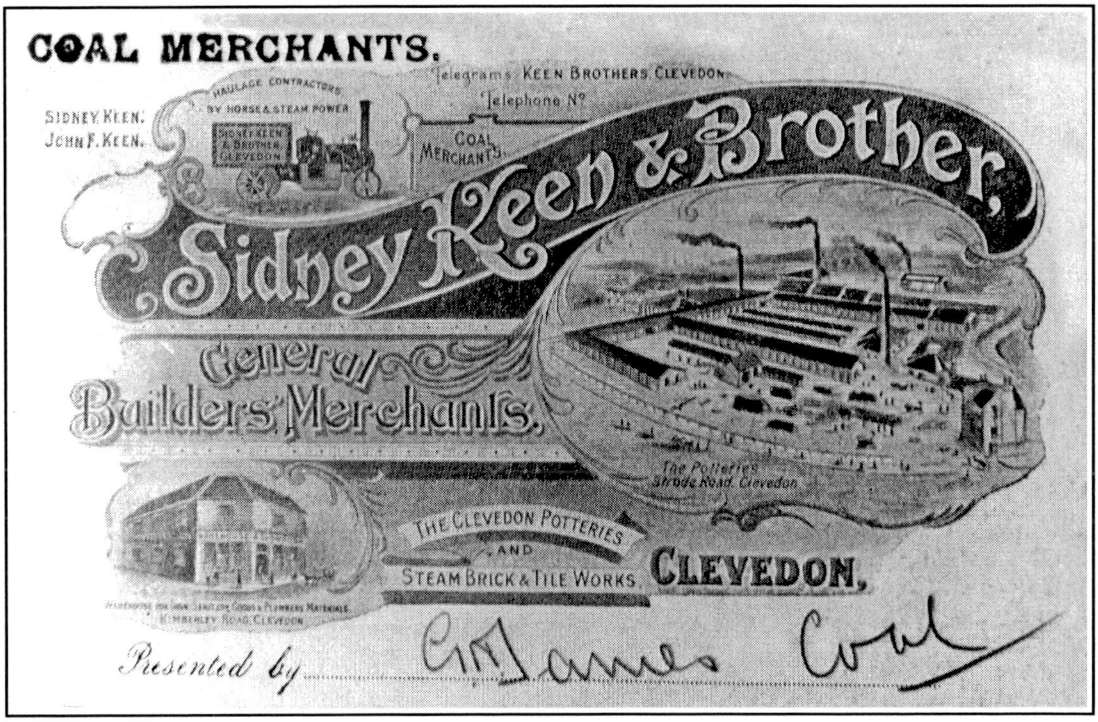
COAL MERCHANTS.
Telegrams, KEEN BROTHERS, CLEVEDON.
Telephone No
HAULAGE CONTRACTORS BY HORSE & STEAM POWER
SIDNEY KEEN. JOHN F. KEEN.
COAL MERCHANTS.
Sidney Keen & Brother,
General Builders' Merchants.
The Potteries Strode Road, Clevedon
THE CLEVEDON POTTERIES AND STEAM BRICK & TILE WORKS.
CLEVEDON,
KIMBERLEY ROAD, CLEVEDON
Presented by
G H James Coal

Kenn Road Brickworks

I have also been unable to find out when these brickworks began - dates are elusive with businesses, it seems; but they were certainly established by 1884, when they are shown on the large scale OS. map of Clevedon. Edmund Shopland, who later owned the sawmills in Teignmouth Road, started work here when he left school. He was born in 1872, and would have left school in his early to mid teens, but this doesn't take the date any further back for us, unfortunately.

The certainty is that they were owned and run by the Shopland brothers, William, Charles, John and William's son Edmund until 1898, when they sold the works to Sidney Keen. The deed of sale is a fascinating document, giving us a list of all the equipment used in brick production at that time. The works were to be completely dismantled over a period of five months, for Mr Keen to take away and use in the Strode Road brickworks. There was a traction engine - of course, as we ARE talking about the Shoplands here, great steam enthusiasts - various stationary engines and pumps, and a boiler. And the brick and tile moulds, work tables, kilns, wheelbarrows, drying racks, and even a machine for pressing flooring squares all had to be ready to be moved to their new home for re-use. The chimney and worksheds were to be taken down, too.

All that was left behind was the office and a stable, together with the bricks from the dismantled chimney. And, of course, the pits from which the clay had been dug. These were backfilled over the years with refuse from the dustbins emptied by the Council, and Hillview Avenue was built on the northern part of the site in the late 1920s. The pit area was left as a playing field for children there. With the rebuilding of Hillview Avenue in the past few years, the old pits were dug out to form foundations, yielding the rubbish of the past to the treasure hunters of the present - unofficially!

After the brickworks came domestic potteries, the earliest in my timespan being the Kenn Road Pottery.

Kenn Road Pottery

The pottery in Kenn Road was at number 34 in the late part of the last century, owned by Mr Charles H Lewis. His associate, Mr Rolling, is standing in the centre of the first photograph of the three I have used here. In the 1897 directory, they are highlighted as being garden pottery manufacturers, but produced many other items fashionable at the time, cast in moulds which were probably widely available. These you can see in the second photograph, showing the range of goods produced. They also produced tiles used to decorate the bay windows of houses in the town, notably the block of three houses, 38-42 Kenn Road, where faces, possibly of Victorian characters such as Florence Nightingale and General Kitchener, still gaze out into the present day. The wide range of ornamental work they made can be seen here. In the third picture is the pugging mill in action, getting the clay smooth and forcing grit out of it. Grit would make the work explode in the kiln, which must have been frustrating in the least! When the pottery closed, just before the World War I, the potter went to work at the brickworks in Strode Road, run by Sidney Keen.

Kenn Road Pottery, Mr Rollings centre

Some of the range of items produced at Kenn Road Pottery

Kenn Road Pottery - Pugging Mill in action

Eltonware

It was in December 1879 that Edmund Elton, as he then was, began to experiment with making pottery. At that time he was living in Highdale Road in a house called Firwood, since re-named The Old Dower House. His early experiments were discouraging, but he persisted with great determination, building and rebuilding kilns, experimenting with glazes and teaching George Masters, a local boy, to turn pots for him on the wheel.

The clay body he perfected is uncommonly dense earthenware, made of local clay mixed with Rockingham clay, sieved together and pounded smooth before use. He began work with an enamelling kiln, but changed to the use of saggars, porous containers used within the kiln to produce even distribution of heat. The pots are stacked inside the saggars.

His designs were remarkable, incorporating twisting dragons, flowers, snakes and birds. But his great achievement lay in his glazes. In 1902 he introduced crackle glazes using platinum and gold, calling the results, 'blue platinum crackle', 'gold crackle', bright platinum crackle' and fiery platinum'. The combination of metallic lustres and the crazed finish made a terrific impression on Victorian society, and these glazes are highly sought after today by collectors of Eltonware.

Besides working in his pottery, Sir Edmund, as he became in 1883, founded the local Fire Brigade, served on the Local Board of Health, was High Sheriff of Somerset, joined the local Volunteers, and was an officer of many clubs and organisations in Clevedon. Not to mention overseeing the administration of his estate and acting as a JP. Beside making his small, decorative pieces, he presented local churches with his work. All Saints, Clevedon, SS Quiricus and Julietta in Tickenham benefited from his generosity.

Sir Edmund died in 1920, aged 74, having been a prodigious worker all his life. He was buried at All Saints' Church, taken there from Clevedon Court on the town's fire engine, drawn by his colleagues and friends in the Brigade that he initiated.

His largest and most public work, and in a way, his finest memorial, is the Clock Tower in Clevedon Triangle, which he embellished with his mosaics and pillars and tiles as a gift to the town to mark the year of Queen Victoria's Diamond Jubilee. The best collection on public display is at Clevedon Court.

Holland's Clevedon Pottery

The first venture to include household and decorative wares was set up by William Fishley Holland, who came to Clevedon initially to help with the making of Eltonware.

William Fishley Holland came of a family associated with pottery in the Fremington and Barnstaple areas of North Devon for five generations. The first known potter in the family was born as long ago as 1770, and from his confident style and excellent products, it is tempting to assume that there were potters farther back in the family than that. His mother was the daughter of Edwin Beer Fishley, who owned the pottery, and his father was a farmer, who died when William was a child, leaving his mother

William Holland with George Holland and Isobel

to run a farm and bring up five young children. At the age of ten, he went to Appledore to work in his uncle's grocery shop, then at fourteen moved to the pottery and began his training making plant pots. This was in 1903.

In 1912, E B Fishley died. The pottery had to be evenly divided between his four children. For a while, WFH worked for his uncles, but eventually the pottery was sold over his head. This meant that W F Holland had to look for work on his own account, which he eventually found as manager at the newly set up pottery at Braunton. He says in his autobiography, 'Fifty Years a Potter', that he was not worried that he was not mentioned in the Will, but that Edwin B Fishley had left him with, 'the ability to earn a living, the memory of a great craftsman and a grandfather to be proud of'.

At Braunton, WFH used his time well, learning how to produce brightly coloured, slip decorated pots, some modelled on pottery brought back from Europe by interested tourists before the Great War broke out.

He developed a clear green and a bright blue glaze, making pots for Henry Williamson, the author. At this time he trained Amy Krauss, who later potted at Corfe Castle. A better known name to pottery collectors will be that of Michael Cardew. His family visited Fremington every summer, and he came to Braunton to learn from WFH how to turn pots on the wheel. In an interview given on his eightieth birthday, he revealed that, when he visited Fremington to watch old Mr Fishley, he would kick the shins of anyone who tried to take him away!

On WFH's return from War service, he found that there was a higher and higher demand for bright colours - a similar reaction, curiously, set in after the Second War, too. From pottery he made at both Braunton and Clevedon I have collected orange, brown, mustard, custard yellow, turquoise, pale green, emerald green, sage green, pink, maroon, crimson, cobalt blue, powder blue, black... the list is impressive! These colours gave way to more subdued shades after a Factory Act forbad the use of lead as a flux in firing, giving the colours most people associate with the Clevedon Pottery of grey, pale green, brown, maroon and turquoise.

The pottery at Braunton had to be sold after the owners had financial problems in 1920. It was now that WFH had the opportunity to come to Clevedon, working for Sir Ambrose Elton. Sir Ambrose was trying to continue the work of his father, Sir Edmund, 'the Potter Baronet', but after the death of George Masters had no-one who could throw any pots for him. WFH would work for the Sunflower Pottery at the Court for one day, and make his own pots there the rest of the time. It was at this time that he was offered the chance to work with the late Bernard Leach at St. Ives, but decided to go on working on his own, as he had always done. Leach frequently came to Clevedon to chat with WFH and watch him at work - they enjoyed each other's company very much.

The arrangement with the Sunflower Pottery did not last long. Indeed, it died with the pottery itself. Art pottery as a type was giving way to studio pottery, and peasant pottery was undergoing a revival. With the help of George Manley, who moved with him from Braunton, WFH set up his own kiln near the orchard of his house in Court Lane, at first digging his own clay on site, then sending to Barnstaple for clay from the Fremington clay seam. When he set up the pottery, he would have been surprised to know what a local institution it would become, welcoming visitors from all over the world for the duration of its long life. Clevedon Pottery outlasted WFH himself - he died in 1969 - continuing in the family until 1977, when it was sold to Norman Darby. Mr Darby produced stoneware there until he had to retire from ill health a short few years later. Now, Sheldon Pottery is run on the site; the owner, John Bishop, trained at Clevedon Pottery in the sixties with his brothers, Charles and David. WFH's grandson, Peter, also trained here, is now running his own pottery in Jedburgh, on the Borders. The woodfired kiln you can see at the pottery is one that he built and used before the pottery was sold in 1977.

The photograph *(page 11)* was taken in the mid-twenties. It shows Isabel Holland, seated, decorating - her talent was in the making of figurines, brightly coloured, jolly pieces. Her father, William Fishley Holland is standing behind her, putting the handle on a chamber candlestick. The young man is George Fishley Holland, one of his two sons. George moved to Dunster Pottery in the mid-fifties, and now still does a little teaching at Minehead.

Sheldon Pottery

This pottery began in the Cinema Buildings on June 1st, 1970, set up by John and David Bishop, who had both previously worked for the Hollands in Court Lane.

John Bishop first worked at the old pottery when he left school in 1960. Three years later, his younger brother David joined him at Holland's, and they remember most of the Holland family; William Fishley Holland, his son William (Bill) and grandson Peter. Staff generally stayed for a long time at the Pottery, and they remember George Manley too, who had then been there since the early twenties. At the time when they joined the pottery, William Fishley Holland was still turning a surprising number of pots on the wheel for a man in his seventies!

John and David took a while to decide on a name for their pottery when they left Hollands. After some discussion, they chose John's second name, Sheldon. One suggestion was Yeo Pottery, which John turned down as rather 'folksy'. It would have suited, with the Land Yeo at the back of the cinema - in fact, it was chosen as a name by Bill Janes in 1977, when he set up his pottery on the same river in Moor Lane. John would like to have had the town name, but Mr Holland had already called his work, Clevedon Pottery. Ironically, this name was not officially registered until the Holland family sold their business in 1977, and could have been used by almost anyone!

The part of the Cinema Buildings they used now fronts Great Western Road, and was the old stable building used by the horsecabs. When they moved in, the tethering rings and hooks for the horses' hay bags were still in place. Now the shop sells second-hand furniture. They began with two electric kilns, buying a third and then a fourth when they took on a massive amount of wholesale work about 18 months after opening. This influx of work meant that they could afford to take on their youngest brother, Charles. They produced up to four kilns of decorated earthenware per day, six days a week at times - John recalls electricity bills peaking at £900 a quarter, the equivalent now being ten times that in present day values!

Most of their work was produced for a Birmingham wholesaler, Desmond Cooper and Company. Desmond was a dapper man in his early eighties, who enjoyed keeping his hand in visiting suppliers even in his retirement. His brother, Melville, played the Sheriff of Nottingham opposite Errol Flynn in Robin Hood. The firm was sold, however, in the late seventies, and the new owners dropped hand made pottery as a line overnight. This was a blow to the business, which needed new outlets for work. Locals bought lines, and commissioned plates for special occasions, but outside orders are always a great help to small craft businesses. David left the pottery, then Charles was unable to work because of illness.

John continued at the old site until 1990, when he moved to take premises at the old Clevedon Pottery in Court Lane, which had become a craft centre. The pottery buildings and house have been much extended and renovated, and bear little resemblance to the place the Hollands knew. Other than cast cement garden tubs, John's pottery is the only work made on the premises. Most of his work is still made for wholesalers, and special orders fill the shelves, too, for schools, clubs and organisations. Keep an eye open for Sheldon Pottery when visiting the shops on holiday, it's very popular.

Yeo Pottery

Like Sheldon Pottery, Yeo Pottery was formed by people who worked at the Clevedon Pottery in Court Lane. In 1977, when the Clevedon Pottery closed, the Yeo Pottery opened in October around the corner in Moor Lane. When I had a collection of local pottery, I could always date the end of one pottery and the beginning of the other from the Queen's Jubilee of 1977; I had commemorative mugs for the event decorated by Bill Janes from both Clevedon Pottery and Yeo Pottery.

Bill Janes had been decorating pottery for William Fishley Holland for more than twenty years when the old pottery closed. He lived in Moor Lane, opposite the Craft Centre, with space for workshops there, so he set up on his own with Andrew Gooding, who also worked at the Clevedon Pottery.

The new pottery was called Yeo Pottery, after the Land Yeo river on the other side of the road. Bill decorated Andy's pots with his customary flair, his easy brushwork producing owls, snails, mice, ducks, fish and flowers on the domestic ware and vases they made. He trained Steven Lampert, who took over the day to day decorating work between 1983 and 1993. Like Clevedon Pottery before them, they had the contract for making the souvenir ware decorated with the Glastonbury Thorn. Boxes of the leaves would arrive, put onto pots, burned off in firing to form the pattern or to be dipped with the glaze on top of them and peeled away afterwards, leaving the shape of the leaf behind on the clay. This provided a good basic income from outside; reliable money that the small craftsman needs.

The area had become a good centre for visitors interested in crafts; the Craft Centre had opened in 1966, there was Clevedon Pottery, running as a small craft centre later, too, and now Yeo Pottery, with ducks and chicken running around in the yard under the nose of complacent cats.

Bill Janes died in 1988, and Andrew carried on running the pottery until he had to close in August 1993.

Unfortunately, a new motorway service station was proposed for the area. The cottage had been sold after Bill's death in 1988, and now belonged to the company who wanted to build the service station. Business declined at the same time, and Andrew gave up the pottery. The service station failed to get planning permission, and the cottage has been sold on and is now being renovated. Many visitors still come back years later, expecting to see the display case full of brightly coloured ware, just as people did with Holland's, in Court Lane - these potteries are much missed.

The Beach Pottery

The pottery was set up here by Frank and Fran Benatt. Fran has been potting since 1960, working at Briglin Pottery in London with Brigitta Appleby, and in Denmark. She taught in Wandsworth while at Briglin Pottery, too. When she married Frank Benatt, he was a chemical engineer, but soon found that he enjoyed pottery more than working at RTZ in Avonmouth. After living and potting in Bristol for 5 years, they set up the Beach Pottery in 1972, and Frank continued to work part-time at RTZ while the business was getting on its feet.

The building is ideal for running a pottery, roomy - for a three-generation family - and well sited. In 1986, the Benatts moved to Devon, but kept an outlet for their work in their old showrooms here. In their pottery at Lower Allerton Farmhouse, Dartington, they have more workshop space, and are surrounded by countryside. Their son, Joss, has been potting since he was 14, and seems set to continue. He produces the plates and mugs decorated with domestic and farm animals. Fran decorates with stylish patterns and elegant brushwork. At first the pots were plain, but more and more people asked for decorated pieces, and for years Fran has produced a stunning array of colours and designs. There are many regular customers in Clevedon - I am one, and have been a hopeless addict for years! Work is also sold through the Devon Guild of Craftsmen and in Bristol.

In ancient times, we imported pottery into the town from the surrounding area. There is no evidence of pottery being made in Clevedon before 1800 - which doesn't rule out the possibility that it was made here. There are plenty of pieces of broken pot found on old house sites to indicate that Ham Green ware was used here in the fourteenth century, German saltglaze in the seventeenth century and the striped, combed patterned cooking pots were popular in the sixteenth century and afterwards. Roofing consisted of reed thatch locally, with the occasional exception of a stone roof, as as Highdale Farm. We were lucky in having plenty of stone for building, so a shortage of bricks was not an insurmountable problem.

In my lifetime, I have seen the potters working at Hollands Pottery in Court Lane, and been privileged to watch the founding of Sheldon Pottery in 1970, the Beach Pottery in 1972 and Yeo Pottery in 1977. Though potteries have come and gone, I hope that the remaining ones will prosper well beyond the millennium.

Jane Lilly

❑ ❑ ❑ ❑ ❑

Weaving in Clevedon

The earliest traces of commercial weaving relevant to Clevedon are to be found in the existence of the Tucking Mills on the Land Yeo below Clevedon Court. Weaving took place in Bristol under the auspices of the powerful Guilds - the Trade Unions of their day. But the cloth was brought south into the villages where clean stream water was available for tucking or fulling. The Land Yeo was used to dampen the cloth, and to power the mills. These were hammers set on eccentric cams, and it was someone's monotonous task to move the wet cloth about under the hammers as they pounded away all day. This thickened the weave of the cloth; it was said that cloth from Bristol needed no stitching round the buttonholes of even waistcoats, it was made so strong by this fulling. The first reference to the mills is in the Wake Survey of 1630, when they are listed as part of the 'demesne' properties, directly rented out from the Lord of the Manor. At that time they were valued at £3/10/- a year, or £3.50p. It is not known when they fell into disuse, but by the end of the 17th century, the Cotswolds led the wool trade instead of Somerset. John de Clevedon, Lord of the Manor until 1346, was responsible for reporting the amount of wool exported from Somerset during the year 1342. He returned a frivolous answer and the King fined him!

Another John de Clevedon, from a branch of the family settled in South Somerset, was exporting cloth from Bristol in 1390, on a ship called the 'Jonet'. Journeying forward in time to the year 1907, weaving itself took place in Clevedon in Gardens Road. The Misses Kate Button and Margaret Lloyd took over what is still known as 'Weaver's House'. The building began its life as a butcher's shop in the 1860s, but its larger, north facing windows made it ideal for craft workshops. It is now made into office accommodation. The original idea of the business was to provide healthy and interesting work for women. It was a deliberate policy that less physically able girls should be taken on so that they could learn a trade and be self-supporting. As well as paid girls, there were pupils who paid for their lessons. They could be taught about spinning flax and wool,

tapestry and shuttle weaving and so forth. The advertisement says, 'Spinning and weaving form a valuable asset to those going to the Colonies, or taking up mission work abroad.' The work undertaken was extremely varied, including tapestries, carpets, pictorial hangings, architects' designs for curtains, wall decorations, carpets, costume cloths, blouse materials and many other art fabrics. To quote their advertisement again, 'the Industry holds the Silver Medals for Cloth and Tapestry Weaving, awarded by the judges at the Franco-British Exhibition in 1918, and the Medal of the Somerset Arts and Crafts Association for 1909, also a Gold Medal awarded at the Coronation Exhibition, 1911. No visitor to Clevedon should fail to inspect this interesting industry, and see the work in progress at the Workshops, Gardens Road and Alexandra Road, between the hours of 10 to 1pm and 2.30 to 4.30pm. Saturdays, 10 am to 12.30pm.' Miss Grayson went into partnership with Miss Lloyd and Miss Button, and then in partnership with her sister, Mrs Greenwell-Lax, bought the business from them. She was Principal herself until 1946. In 1981, I was lucky enough to meet one of the girls trained by Miss Grayson, Zena Hart, nee Hill. The text which follows came from her conversation with me. Zena's information was published in the Clevedon Mercury as part of the Village Pump series after her sudden and unexpected death a few weeks after I spoke to her. Zena Hart was one of the Weavers from 1923 until she left in 1928 to marry Jack Hart of Nailsea. Zena remembered the workshops very well, and this is what she told me about her work there. Going in through the rear of the building, below street level, the wool store was to the right. Through this room was the weaving room, with double and single width looms for tweed, and a single-width loom for linen. The silk and cotton store was in the right hand corner of this room. The dyeing room, where many natural dyestuffs were used, was next to the silk and cotton store. Upstairs, at street level, was the shop/showroom, with two big looms. There was a big wheel for twisting cords, a Welsh spinning wheel and a Scandinavian wheel, together with two Saxony wheels. For church work there was a tapestry loom with carved pillars, about seven feet high. In the long room next to this one were the silks and display cabinets. The white and blue silk was to the left and the black, gold and peacock silk to the right. There was a scarf loom and a small tapestry loom against the wall, and a stand of tweed in rolls. The larger of the two display cabinets was used for silks, cottons and scarves, and the smaller one was filled with the Indian brassware brought back by Dr and Mrs Greenwell-Lax. This was kept shining with banana oil. When Zena started work here at the age of almost fifteen the first task she took up was sorting a tangled mass of threads

into shades and colours. Miss Grayson having established that she could do this correctly, she was afterwards taught spinning, carding, combing and how to make heddles for the looms. She was then taught weaving, beginning with making the warps, done on a warping mill. The threads had to be put through the holes in the heddles, then through the comb-like reed and then tied down. Silk warps were 100 yards long, and there were 1,760 threads to a width. So by the time you had threaded a loom for silk, you had used 100 miles of fine thread. The pattern of the cloth was governed by the heddles which were lifted when the feet pushed the pedals called lams. As the warp ran out, more thread was tied on to save threading up all over again, and to conserve materials. The last piece of work Zena made at Somerset Weavers before she left was for Countess Dillon, who had commissioned a length of black and white floral silk wool mix. She wanted about 10 yards for an evening dress and wrap. The cloth was made to a high standard, for Miss Grayson expected to be able to use a gauge anywhere on the finished length and find that all the threads were true and woven to the correct density. The gauge magnified and area of cloth half an inch by a quarter of an inch! Countess Dillon commended the weaving very highly in her letter to Miss Grayson saying that the length had been received. The other girls working with Zena during her time there were Miss Cambridge, Susan Hamlin, Doris Meade-Oliver, Margaret Kent, Miss Hyacinth Orde, Miss Nettie Douglas, Miss King and Miss Gertrude Barnes. Also Winnie Moir and Peggy Ware. Something Zena told me that I left out of this when it was written was that when the girls were learning to spin with spindles they used

The Somerset Weavers, Clevedon

to go and sit on the high wall by Christ Church in Highdale Road and see whose spindles would reach the ground far below first, without snapping the thread! All those young girls must have had a lovely time dangling their legs over the wall in the open air. As a result of the article in the Mercury, I was delighted to hear from the last girl employed by the Weavers, Mrs G E Edwards, nee Gallop, living in Yatton. She remembered the workshops producing hangings for the church at Weston Zoyland, of blue and grey, it being her lot as the youngest girls to blend the colours for the bobbins. Her sister, Vi, went to the Ideal Home Exhibition with Miss Grayson to man the Weavers' trade stand there. The two items which Mrs Edwards recalled most clearly were a pure silk shawl square in blues and greens, and a white lambs' wool and silver thread shawl. This last item was bought by Queen Mary herself. The Weavers did not long outlast the War, having battled on through shortages of materials. Here is an article from the Mercury of August 3rd, 1946:-

"Miss L G Grayson, Principal of Somerset Weavers, Gardens Road, after being responsible for the industry for nearly forty years, has recently retired. During her long connection Miss Grayson has gained for the industry a national reputation for the excellency of its work, and as a consequence many awards were obtained at exhibitions, both in this country and abroad. Members of the Royal Family have been amongst its patrons. Her post as Principal has been filled by Miss Aileen Smith of Crawley, Sussex, who was previously Miss Grayson's assistant for six years. Miss Grayson, who is one of the oldest members of the National Savings Movement, has resigned the Secretaryship of the Somerset Weavers Group which she started in 1917."

The accompanying postcard illustration *(page 19)* shows most of the staff at work, dressed in blue overalls.

Jane Lilly

❑ ❑ ❑ ❑ ❑

Mr Woodington's Boot Factory

Mr. Woodington & his wife Alice were the owners of what in former times was known as "The Boot Factory" and in the 1920's and early 1930's it was the only large industry in the town. Employees at the factory not only came from Clevedon, but both men and women came from Nailsea and Portishead. One skilled leather cutter actually commuted daily from Kingswood. First catching a bus from Kingswood to Temple Meads railway station, train to Clevedon, then the walk across the footpath to the factory and, to make matters more difficult, he was a crippled gentleman. To my memory he was never late for work.

It has been impossible for me to define the exact date when the "Clevedon Enterprise" started, but I do know, that a planning application was made to build a factory and houses in lower Strode Road in 1896 and 2 years later, a further application was lodged for an extension to the factory. It is believed, from information given me by my 'old boss', Mr. Tom Roynon, that at the time when this planning application was submitted, there was certain opposition in the town, by some residents who did not like the idea of "factory workers". They thought it would lower the town's prestige. In my years with Woodington's, I well remember an Illustrated Certificate of loyalty, hanging in the Private Office, signed by the founder employees who started the "Clevedon Factory" and who came from the Woodington's Factory in St. George, Bristol.

But, to go back to the origins of the J. H. Woodington Empire, we have to go to a date even before the 1890's, because Mr. Woodington owned a factory at St. George, Bristol, of similar size to the one in Clevedon, whose main product was boys and girls school boots. Yes, girls wore boots similar to boys in those days, except that they did not have hob-nails in the soles, but cutlan nails, which were driven in flush with the sole.

In order to enlarge his production, the Clevedon factory was built, together with a row of factory cottages (Sea View Terrace) and to get manufacturing started he brought with him from St. George Factory, "key workers" in order to teach

Skilled operatives were brought down from the Bristol factories.

the new employees at Clevedon. These "key-workers" being housed in "Sea View Terrace". So the "Clevedon Enterprise," was off the ground and from information given me by some of the ex Bristol employees, it was to become a very important factor to the economy of Clevedon. The labour force at that time was around 100 people, the population of Clevedon being about 5000, so one could say that Mr. Woodington employed about 2% of the local population. Before 1914, a business connection was established with South Africa which helped the factory to have full-time employment, as without this export business, there could be no guarantee, of this, as heavy working boots were really a seasonal trade. Tom Roynon, the factory manager who later taught me my profession, often told me about the times when the local trades-people contacted him to know how our order books stood, in order that they could budget their stocks accordingly. Short time working, meant less money to spend on the necessities of life.

For me the dates are uncertain, but after the first World War we had the big depression here in England, the factory was closed for a period and it was only restarted by an arrangement with the "Labour Exchange" when the people worked for 3 days and signed on for 3 days. How the "signing on" helped them financially is unclear, but there must have been some financial arrangement. I believe, it had something to do with the number of "unemployment stamps" they were able to have on their "dole card" in order to qualify for "dole money".

Hard times.

Then, as we came out of the depression, the working hours increased until they were back to the full week of 52 hours !!!!! Before the depression, the working week was even longer. Once again, from information given me in my early years with the company, original employees told me that the men started at 6am, breaking off for half an hour (7-30 - 8am) for breakfast. In fact, behind the garage and leather store at the east side (rear) of the factory, there was a small building which was the breakfast room, especially built for this purpose. Halfday, was Saturday 4pm.!!!

In October 1934, when I started with the Company as "office boy" my hours were 8am to 6-30pm, Saturday 8am to 1pm, but first I had to go the the General Post Office in Hill Road, to collect the Company's mail and be at the factory by 8am. In the evening 6-30pm often meant 7pm, when I had to go again to the General Post Office to deliver the out-going mail, (neatly tied in bundles) to the sorting office.

It is uncertain when the factory at Chesham, Bucks was opened, but Mr. Woodington had a plant there making footwear of a higher quality. I have little knowledge as to when it opened or when it closed, but I do know that it was sold or leased to a company around 1938, called the "Spa Brush Company".

As well as the factory at St. George, there was also one at "Mardyke" Bristol, opposite what was then known as the "Flying Fox" in Hotwells. This factory produced the "cut-soles" and heel pieces for both St. George and Clevedon and of course, in those days they were 100%

leather. Mardyke was totally destroyed in a bombing raid during the war and never rebuilt. Their part of the production being carried on in the respective factories of St. George and Clevedon.

Since writing this, I have been given some further information, which may be of interest and was supplied by:-

R. Criddle, Standish Close,
Henbury. Bristol.

It is as follows:-

"From researches in the *Wrights Bristol Directory* for 1915 it has been discovered that Clifton Certified Industrial School, Hotwell Road, housed 175 boys, supported by contributions with allowances for boys sent under the Act. The main entrance was in Church Path Steps and the Head-master was John Edgar Wilshaw. It is believed this building changed to Woodington's leather & shoe factory after the First World War." So now we have some more information.

Mr. Woodington also owned a leather tannery in Bristol, known as "Waterloo Leather Works". I have, little knowledge of its production and to me, it did not appear to be of great importance to the production of footwear in the Woodington Empire.

Now we come to "Sunhill", Mr & Mrs Woodington's private residence in Clevedon, which is now owned by Woodspring District Council and is used as the Clevedon Community Centre. Of course, I am referring to the "old" part of the Community Centre and not the building extension formally known as the the "New Hall" and now, "Princes Hall".

To the south side of the house were lawns and the "Tropical Houses" which in their heyday were a wonderful sight. To the west side was lawn, tennis court and bowling green and to the east side, vegetable gardens. Also to the south side were the carnation houses, (I believe 2). Every morning 365 days in the year, the head gardener had to go to the main house and present on a silver tray, 3 carnations from which Mr. Woodington (or in his absence) Mrs. Woodington, could select one for his button-hole. As Mr. Fred Avis (the head gardener) once told me, it was more than his job was worth, not to present 3 carnations that were not in tip-top condition and I believed him. It was always the small matters that were so important to Joey (as he was known). He could and did, fly off in a terrible rage about things that we might consider of no great importance, Soon after I started work, I was walking through the factory one day and I came face to face with the "Great Man" and when he called me over. I confess my knees started to tremble, wondering what I had done wrong. A piece of string about 12" (30cm) long was lying on the floor, he picked it up and commenced to give me a lecture on waste which lasted about ¼ hour. It was a lesson I have never forgotten.

It is also interesting to note, that disregarding his economies in many things, he was very up-to-date. In 1926, when Clevedon telephone exchange had fewer than 200 subscribers, (which included surrounding villages) he had 2 telephone lines, one at his private address, Telephone Clevedon 5 and the other Clevedon 10, for the factory number, which also had extensions for various offices.

There was another episode which illustrates his determined character and that was regarding our gas supply. From the early days, all machinery in the factory was driven by a single large Crossley Gas Engine with 6ft diameter flywheel, housed in a small building extension on the north side of the factory. Large leather or balata belting was used in conjunction with shaftings at suitable intervals to drive the various machines right across the factory. Early each morning the engine was started (in free wheel) and then by the use of free and fixed wheel pulleys, the various shaftings were engaged until everything was running. If for any reason, the engine stopped or faltered there was a panic to get the free wheel pulleys running in order to disengage the shaftings so the engine could be re-started. If this happened when Mr. Woodington was around he became agitated and would demand to know why it happened. The stock answer was from Albert Hailes, the engineer:- "Bad patch of gas". Who could prove otherwise? He was worried about loss of production and seconds or a single nail meant life or death to him. One day this happened several times and being a Director of the Clevedon Gas Company, he was hot foot on the phone to them. Not getting a satisfactory answer, he said he would install his own gas plant, which he then did. It did not last for long and he was soon back with the Clevedon Gas Company. He found out that making gas was more trouble than it was worth. The engine was eventually replaced by having electric motors driving the shafts then, later on, individual electric motors to each machine.

On the other hand, he did have his sentimental side. His one and only child, a daughter, whose name was Kathryn Sybil, (addressed by the staff as Miss Sybil) died of meningitis and was buried on the 31st October 1919, at the tender age of 16 years. She had been given a car by her father and was in the process of learning to drive. On her death, her father forbade anyone to touch the car and it mouldered away in the garage at the rear of the factory.

From about 1930 onwards, production increased with exports to South Africa, Rhodesia and Ireland, but with South Africa and Rhodesia, this business quickly declined, as they built their own factories and manufactured their own. The trade with Ireland, in those days known as I.F.S. ***(Irish Free State)*** increased to such an extent, that the idea of building a factory there was examined. In those days there were import tariffs as well as freight costs to be taken into consideration and finally, with a subsidy from the Irish Government, (to help with their huge unemployment problem) it was decided to go ahead with the idea at a town called Drogheda. A large building that had been originally constructed for meat processing and which had been empty since its construction, was taken over (I believe it was purchased) and that is how J. H. Woodington (Drogheda) Ltd., started. In order to get this project off the ground, it was necessary to send volunteer labour from various departments at Clevedon to go to Drogheda and help train the new labour force with the skills they required. As to be expected, romances developed and marriages followed. Over the next several years, I believe, all the Clevedon people returned, some with their new found partners in marriage.

During this period, production was building up and eventually included "Army Boots" for H. M. Government, which necessitated Government Inspectors examining all the footwear we made for them. There could be some tales about these "gentlemen" but I think I had better censor them.

The Irish enterprise appeared to be thriving to such an extent that Mr. Woodington decided to extend his "Empire" even further and he started a Tannery at Gorey, Co. Wexford. With all these various factories, there was a lot of correspondence going on between us. Letters, telegrams, telephone calls and being "office boy" I saw and heard a lot of it. Mr. Woodington was a small man in stature but be could be a proper "Spitfire" as many found to their cost. There was no such thing as "unfair dismissal" in those days.

Now came 1939 and WAR. Being in the Territorial Army and having added two years to my age on enlistment, I was mobilised. Except for occasional visits to the "office" when on leave, I have little knowledge of the Clevedon factory during wartime, but since all those employees of military age were "called up" (no reserved occupation here), I was told that the Ministry of Supply kept the factory in production for 2 reasons. The footwear they produced was required for the war effort and the few older people left behind were not of great help to other industries in the area. In addition the Ministry requisitioned about half the factory space for Government use (I have no knowledge as to what this was) so footwear production was very low.

During the war, Mr. Woodington died (he was already an elderly gentleman) and his wife Alice, together with her brother Mr. Pollinger, who had been in the business before his retirement and before my time, continued to run the "Empire". After the war, January 1946 to be exact, I returned to the Company and made my acquaintance with Mr. Pollinger, whom I found to be extremely helpful and very wise. Now, as a married man, I was no longer the "office boy" but was told that I was to understudy the factory manager, Mr. Tom Roynon, with a view to taking over from him in about 5 years time when be was expecting to retire.

At that time, the Ministry released the requisitioned half of the factory and a massive re-organisation was in progress. Order books were full and production was stepped up as quickly as possible, bearing in mind it was very difficult to get supplies as every industry was in the same boat as ourselves, shortage of supplies and leather was still on government licence, in other words we were strictly rationed.

When the Korean war started, England was really caught with its pants down. The Government had sold off so called "war surplus" including military footwear, so panic stations - and we were back to Government contracts and Government Inspectors!!!

At that time, there was a very interesting development in Military Footwear. Soldiers fighting in Korea were having so much trouble with frostbite of the feet, that SATRA (Shoe & Allied Trades Research Association) developed a special "in-sock" to be placed in the army boot, so as to go between the wearer's socked foot and the leather insole of the boot. The special sock can best be described as looking as though it had been made from shredded wheat. What it actually did, was to allow air to circulate between the wearer's foot and the leather insole. The problem was solved.

Mrs. Woodington died and was buried in the Churchyard at St. Andrew's Church, Clevedon on the 5th August 1947 and the "Empire" had to be sold. "Sunhill", Mr. & Mrs Woodington's private residence, together with the 2½ acres of grounds in which it stood was purchased by the C.U.D.C. (Clevedon Urban District Council) for £7,225, for what it is today, The Clevedon Community Centre. Two of the former directors, Mr. Raymond Stone (who was Mr. Woodington's nephew) and Mr.Underwood managed to take over the St. George and Clevedon factories and production continued in much the same way. At the St. George factory large quantities of boys' footwear was made for Marks & Spencers and a new development, ladies' sandals with crepe soles which were so sought after, they could not make enough. Later, orders dropped off, difficulties arose, production at St. George ceased and the factory closed. The type of merchandise they had been making was switched to Clevedon, but it was not an easy thing to have the machine operatives one minute handling and making light weight footwear and the next, the real heavy stuff. So eventually, the St. George type of footwear was stopped.

During this period, the state of Israel was being born and through connections, which one of the directors had with Marks & Spencer, Clevedon started making footwear for females in the new state of Israel. They were of a lighter (in weight) type of men's agricultural boot, for girls working on kibbutz. Very large quantities of these boots were made, to strict specifications, "very specially packed" in 10 pair packages, sewn in hessian and surrounded with waterproof paper.

Even in pre-war days, a small amount of footwear was made with external steel toe caps at the Clevedon factory. Safety regulations were not so stringent in those, days and although they gave a degree of protection in post war days, they did not conform to the B.S.I. regulations. People being employed in dangerous occupations where safety footwear was mandatory, insisted on Grade 1, Carbon Steel Toe Caps and this necessitated a different type of manufacture. It was at this time, when we were having problems with Safety Footwear, that SATRA, requested help in manufacturing agricultural and industrial type footwear, with "man-made" soling material, as opposed to leather. Rubber had been tried prewar, but was of little use. It was through this liaison with SATRA that I made friends with one of their technicians, who helped me tremendously with modern methods of manufacture, one of which was the use of synthetic sewing threads. Formerly, only threads made with 100% cotton were used. He also taught me how to come up to date with "Safety Footwear", both with "Inside and Outside Steel Toe Cases" which would pass the Grade, I test and conform to the B.S.I. regulations. This required that a 50lb weight dropped from 3 feet on to the toe of the boot, would still leave sufficient space above the toes for them not to be injured. This was a tremendous step forward for us and about

1953, we secured the contract to supply all the Miners Safety Boots for the National Coal Board, through their agents. For reasons beyond my control and in which I was in no way involved, the Company went into liquidation in April 1956 and that was the end of the "Woodington Empire".

The manufacture of footwear was very strong in the Bristol area both before and after World War II. At one time, there was in excess of 23 factories. Of course, this meant there were also the ancillary factories making adhesives, heel stiffeners, inks and stains, packing boxes, stationery and of course, labour for transport. A very high proportion of the available labour force was in one way or another connected with footwear.

Sadly, this is all in the past, as very, very little footwear is now made in the U.K. but we are not alone in this respect, as most of our European partners have the same experience.

In former times large quantities of "Raw Hides" came from India and South America in either the Wet or Dry Salt condition. They were then tanned and dressed to the various requirements in this country. Since World War II, both of these sources have virtually dried up, as they decided to tan and dress the leather themselves before exporting it to Europe. Finally, they said "NO" to leather exports and decided to make the finished goods, (footwear) themselves.

It is worth mentioning, that the manufacture of footwear and leather goods is very good employment for developing countries, as all the operations involved, can be done by hand if necessary and where labour is cheap it does not pay to mechanise. But they gradually mechanised the more difficult operations, depending upon labour costs. Around 1984, many thousands of simple, pre-war sewing machines were bought by dealers and sent to South America. Post- war surplus sewing machines of a more complicated nature were not wanted and you could not sell them. Anyone familiar with machines will recognise the model Singer 31k which cost £10 each in 1939. In 1984, they were fetching £50 each (secondhand) and were then sold on to South America. Labour over there is cheap, but it doesn't reflect upon the prices we pay in the U.K. for the finished goods!!!! or, I have failed to notice it.

In his day, Mr. Woodington was a household name in Clevedon. Now I doubt if anyone recognises it.

On a more cheerful note, it is nice to know that the present Chairman of the Clevedon Community Association at Mr. Woodington's old home, "Sunhill", Princes Road, has been responsible for the illumination of the Stained Glass Window at the top of the stairs in the main building. How many people remember this was installed in memory of his daughter, **not** as a status symbol in competition with other "up-market" home owners in the town, as some would have us believe? This information was given to me personally by Mrs. Crease, who was and had been the housekeeper for the family for many, many years, when I was making my first visit to the "residence" in late 1934. I had to get some documents signed by Mr. Woodington, whowas not well and unable to come to the factory.

The name on the Stained Glass Window is "MARGUERITE" and is defined in the Universal Dictionary as a garden plant, chrysanthemum, frutescens, native to the Canary Islands, having white or pale yellow flowers. Any of several similar or related plants having daisy like flowers. French, (from Old French) Marguerite, daisy. From Latin margarita, pearl. From Greek margarites, pearl. In the language of "Flowers" the daisy represents:-

INNOCENCE

Mr. & Mrs. Woodington were devout members of the Congregational Church, Hill Road, Clevedon. They are buried in St. Andrew's Churchyard, Clevedon. GRAVE NUMBER 966.

Interred in this grave are:-

Joseph Henry Woodington	d. 1941
Alice Woodington	d. 1947
Kathryn Sybil Woodington	d. 1919

Mervyn Potter

Footnote:

After Woodingtons closed, Mervyn Potter was asked by Richard Draper & Company of Glastonbury to work for them and start a branch factory in Clevedon. This he did at Knowles Road with a staff of three men and ten ladies, which was eventually built up to approximately 100 people, making footwear uppers, sheepskin coats and ladies and gents leather garments. It is interesting to note, that they were possibly the first people to make sheepskin coats on a production line basis and in the 1960's these were very popular. Another first was the mass production of suede and leather Mini Skirts and Boleros, about 100 per day in addition to the other products.

Mervyn moved to Glastonbury in 1969, to take over the position as General Manager of the Company, a position he held until his retirement in 1985.

❑ ❑ ❑ ❑ ❑

Binding and Payne

BINDING & PAYNE ENGINEERING PRODUCTIONS CAM GEARS

A composite title made up of Companies which had their roots in the efforts of one man, Archer Binding.

When Archer Ormonde Binding left the old National School in Clevedon around the end of the 1800's he signed up as an apprentice with Mr.Stephens who was engaged in pioneering the design of motor cars and the petrol engines to go with them in his factory in Clevedon Triangle. (One hundred years on and Stephens cars are still regularly among the first arrivals in Brighton in the annual London To Brighton Run.)

On the completion of his apprenticeship he went to work in Bristol for a while but returned to Clevedon in 1912 and started up his own engineering works at No. 40 Kenn Road. His engineering enthusiasm enabled him to keep his head above the water and gradually over the next two years was building up a successful business. Then came World War One in 1914 and Archer promptly joined the Royal Naval Air Force. His Service career was carried out with the same enthusiasm and his engineering expertise was soon recognised which resulted in him being posted to work on the design of air ships and their engines. Patents for some of his designs and the Air Force Cross presented to him by King George V marked a very fine wartime service.

Binding & Payne's Garage - pre 1939

Returning to Clevedon in 1919 he bought a piece of land in Old Church Road, next to the Curzon Cinema, put up a corrugated iron building in the days before town planners and was in business again. This was the Central Garage & Engineering Works and soon he was joined by a partner, Harry Payne. On the garage side Binding and Payne then became agents for Austin, Morris and imported American Essex cars. An Austin Seven was priced from £135, the Morris Cowley, £148.10s and the Essex was £250 for the Super Six and £275 for the Super Six Sedan.

The engineering part of the business, amongst other things, undertook design and maintenance work for the Clevedon Gas Company, the Water Company, the Brick and Tile Works, Woodington's Boot Factory and the Clevedon and Portishead Laundry.

The Partnership prospered, expanded and eventually the engineering business became Engineering Productions Ltd. A.O.B., as he was known, was soon drawing upon his experience and becoming involved in the aircraft and engine component industry. This required more space and so a new factory was built along Kenn Road.

One of the productions was a range of turbochargers for Perkins diesel engines and another, the manufacture of ball joints and suspension parts for vehicles and this activity caught the eye of Cam Gears, a company in South Wales specialising in power assisted gear boxes. In 1966 Clevedon's Engineering Productions was acquired and became part of Cam Gears and by 1978 the Clevedon factory became one of the largest employers in the town with a turnover of 24 million pounds and over 60% of the output being exported.

Alas, times, methods and materials changed, meaning that the factory in Kenn Road was no longer a viable proposition and it was closed in the late 1980's. The site was bought by Tesco and, where once the front suspension and steering gear for Volvo cars was made, we now wander around trying to steer a shopping trolley.

However the garage side of the partnership continued on its own site in Old Church Road although this too was touched by the aircraft industry during World War II, it becoming a production unit for the Folland Aircraft Company (another story to be followed up). It can be seen from the attached layout sketch that the shape of the building has changed very little over the past 50 years although the petrol pumps and their verandah, seen on the pre-war photograph have disappeared together with the clock and left hand arch.

In 1960 the garage business was bought by the Yeovil based Vincent Group maintaining the Austin, Morris, MG, and Triumph franchises. It evolved into the area's main Rover Dealer, managed by Mr. Mike Stevens who was a former apprentice with Binding and Payne. The Company had its beginnings in the days when a man with a red flag preceded motor vehicles and Archer Binding's skill and foresight ensured that it lasted into the days of the supersonic land speed record.

Roy Girling

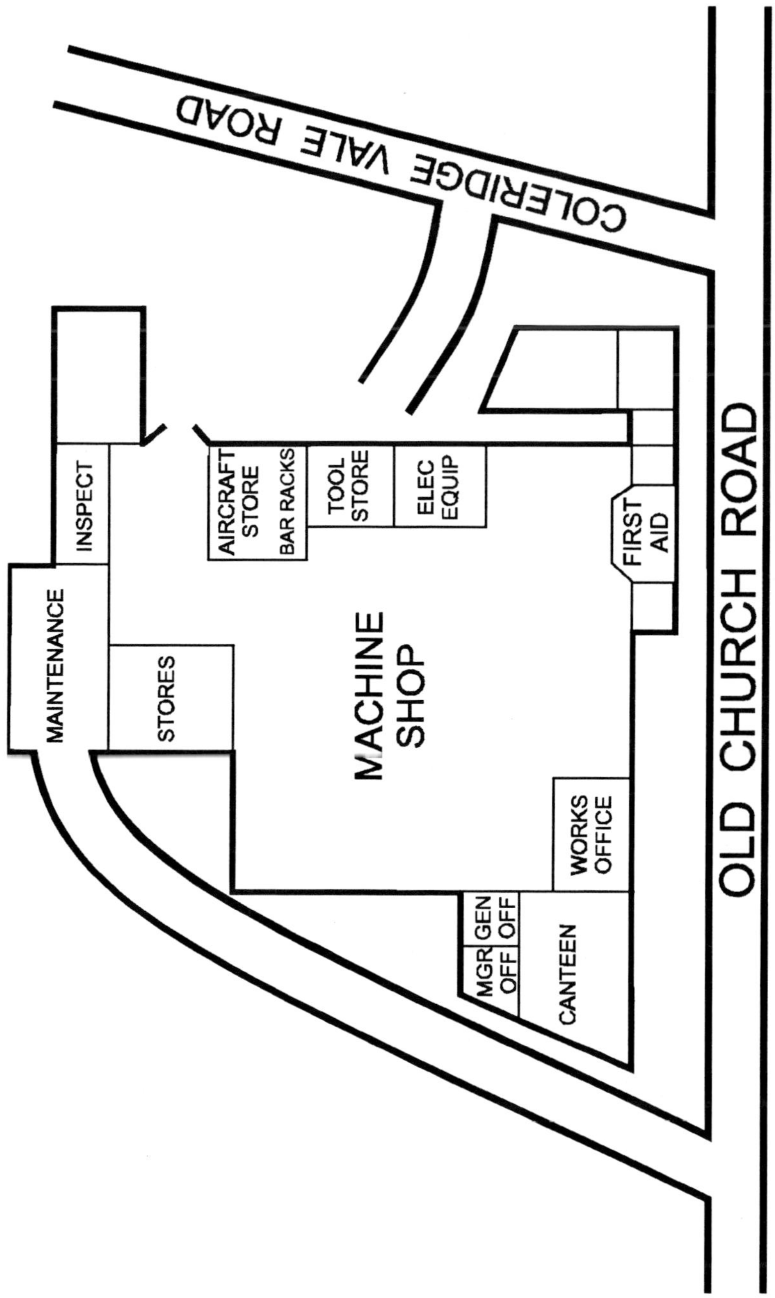

Site Plan of Binding & Payne, Old Church Road, during World War II

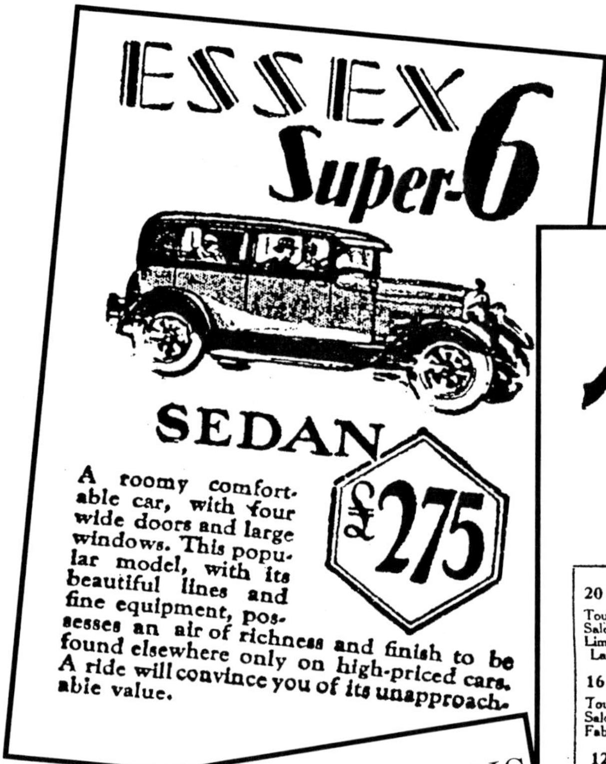

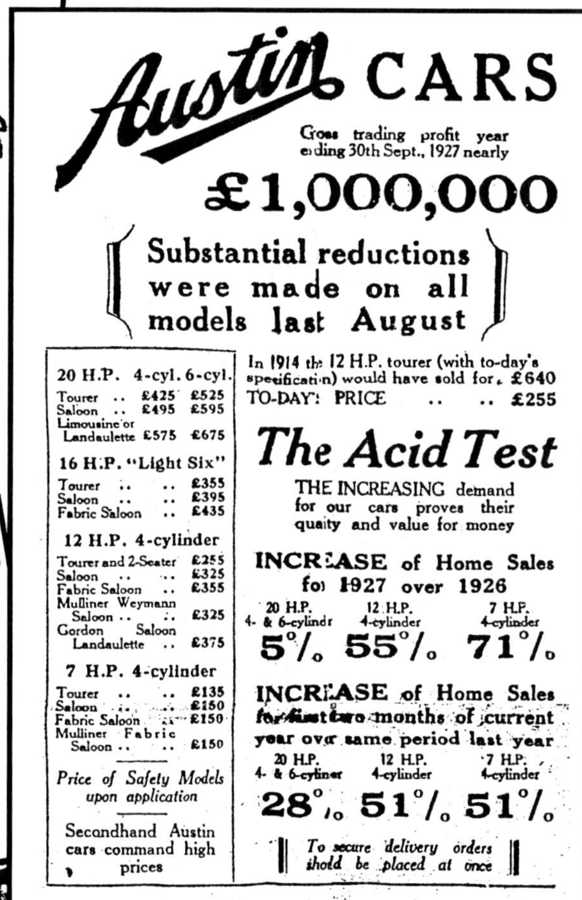

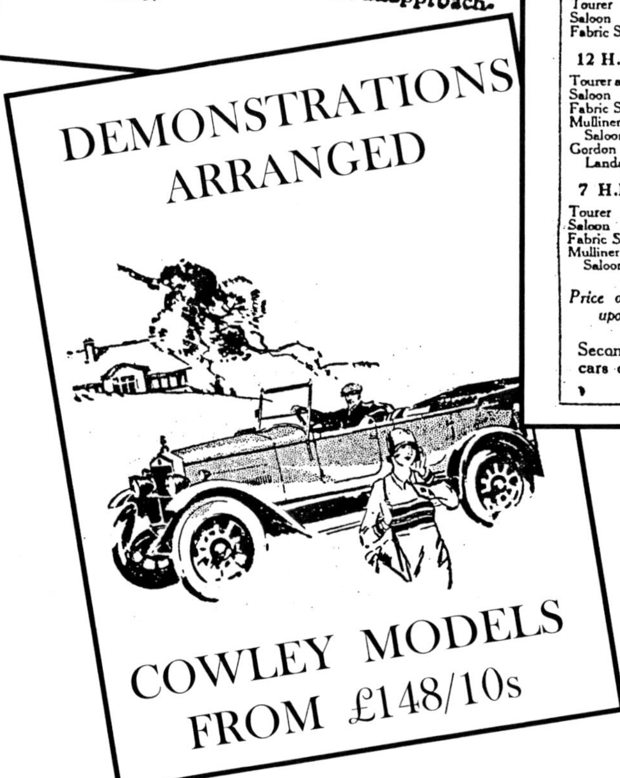

Models available from Binding & Payne, Central Garage, c. 1927

The Clevedon & Portishead Laundry

Another bygone era, a trade virtually wiped out by the washing machine. The weekly visit of the laundry van was a familiar sight in days gone by when the horse drawn vehicle, and later, the motor van came around to deliver clean linen and take away items to be laundered.

Not everyone used the C&P Laundry but the Company was at great pains to point out that theirs was a much superior service to that provided by small 'cottage laundries' as their introductory brochure explains:

"In drawing your attention to the grave dangers arising from the improper manner in which soiled linen is often treated, both as to the mode of treatment as well as to the sanitary conditions prevailing at the place where the linen undergoes treatment, we would respectfully request a perusal of the facts herewith set out"

The brochure goes on to describe how some small cottage laundries, when inspected by Government Inspectors, were found to be infected by contagious diseases, but the Clevedon & Portishead Laundry was purpose designed and equipped with every sanitary arrangement and appliance possible to be procured and was free of such dangers.

The prospective customer was requested to give the Company's service a trial and was further informed that:

"The machinery is up to date, and a minimum of wear and tear is assured, as against the old method of hard scrubbing brushes and boards. The linen is subject only to a gentle roll and squeeze, which, with the aid of pure soap and soda only, effectively removes all dirt and stains.................In conclusion we would beg for a trial, and in such an event to use every endeavour to give you satisfaction."

Exterior view of Laundry

Washhouse

Machine Ironing Room

For the convenience of customers living in Walton and the upper part of the town a depot was established at No. 25 Alexandra Road managed by Miss White. Articles could be left there with any special instructions and an Express Messenger would call daily for orders. For those customers with regular requirements the van made house to house calls in Clevedon, Portishead and surrounding districts and the laundry handled 'thousands of items daily'.

The Laundry was built in Kimberly Road (where the Comet Warehouse is now) in about 1905 in the days of the horse and cart, as can be seen on the exterior view of the site. The Managing Director was Mr. Tony May, who was also M.D. of the Brickworks across the road. The day to day management was carried out by Mr. Chapman with assistance from his Forelady, Ellen Godwin, they are both in the photograph of the stand at a local show. Mr. May's son Nicholas joined the company in 1960 and, on the death of Mr. Chapman, took over as Manager until the final closure of the operation in 1965.

Other photographs show the various activities which took place and a major feature in some of the pictures is the wicker basket which was used for the collection and delivery of the laundry. There appears to be lots of them and one wonders where the all went to, they are virtually indestructible so where are they now?

For several years the five washing drums, the centrifuges for spin drying and the tumbler dryers were driven by belts from

Mr Chapman and Ellen Godwin manning an exhibition stand

overhead pullies which in turn were driven from an engine with a boiler. This also provided the hot water and steam for the washing machines. The belt drive system was later replaced by individual electric motors making for a much safer and quieter working environment.

Now the majority of domestic laundry in Clevedon has become a do-it-yourself activity either by patronising the laundrette or using the washing machine at home and anyone requiring a commercial service has to call on Weston-s-Mare or Bristol.

25 Alexandra Road, Clevedon

Roy Girling

❑ ❑ ❑ ❑ ❑

Percy Daniel & Co. Ltd.

ORGAN BUILDERS

The firm was founded by the late Percy Gordon Eckersley Daniel between the two World Wars. Mr. Daniel had come to Clevedon as a boy when his father was involved in the building of Portishead Docks from 1877 onwards. His interest in music in general and organs in particular, was manifest at an early age when he built his first organ in his bedroom. His reputation spread locally and he opened his first workshop in the red brick building which still stands near the bus stop at East Clevedon opposite Clerical Medical Offices.

It was in this building that he built the organ for St. Benedicts Church at Glastonbury and it turned out to be too tall for the building when it was being finally assembled for testing so a piece had to be cut out of the roof timbers to allow it to fit. The roof is still like that today!

In the mid 1930's, by which time he was employing several craftsmen, he acquired a piece of land at East Clevedon to erect his first purpose-built factory which was enlarged over the years as the firm grew. He could see the factory from his house in Walton Road so could watch his workers come and go and see who was on time and who was late!

These premises were sold in 1993 to make way for industrial expansion and a move was made to a large former joinery workshop in Beach Avenue, Clevedon, having the benefit of an excellent woodworking mill with a comprehensive range of machinery.

Mr. Daniel died at the age of 80 in 1955 and is buried in All Saints Churchyard but the continuity and traditions of his Company are carried on by the present Directors, who, between them have over seventy years service with the Company.

St. Peters Church in Alexandra Road was, before it was re-built in 1958, a metal clad building which had been delivered by rail in 1919, complete with organ, from Kent where it had been the Chapel of the Danehill High School in Cliftonville, Margate. Mr. Daniel's first professional job was the re-assembly, overhaul and installation of that organ into the Church after it too had been re-assembled.

The organ was originally built by August Gern who before setting up his own organ building business in England, had been the foreman of Cavaillé-Coll a famous French organ builder.

From this start Mr.Daniel went on to build organs as well as overhaul, restore and tune them.

There was a spate of organ building from 1880 to 1920 but now with so many Churches closing the accent is on moving organs from one place to another. So typically an organ from Minehead goes to Chippenham and one from Lockleaze goes to Alveston, therefore the skills of the organ builder are still very much in demand.

A staff of 14 is kept busy with 3 members continuously "on the road" tuning organs from Devon to Kent, the London area, South Wales, through the Midlands up to Leeds. Overhauls may be carried out 'in situ' but where major work is required all the working parts of the organ are brought to the Beach Avenue workshop for thorough cleaning and restoration. In these days of electronics and micro-chips 90% of organs still have mechanical actions for reliability and when Daniel's can give the finished job a TWENTY YEAR guarantee there must be a message in there somewhere! Restoration may take up to 3 months to complete, and although the organ pipes, of which there can be up to 1200, are usually not brought to Clevedon they are checked over and replaced or repaired where necessary.

The round metal pipes which are the usual visual feature of an organ are made from an alloy of 60% tin and 40% lead. This metal is made in sheets and then cut to size, rolled around a mandrel and soldered along the seam. The City of Leeds in Yorkshire is where Daniel & Co. go for replacements as that is where most of the basic metal pipes are made. The fine work in finishing and tuning the new pipes is then carried out by the Company in Clevedon. The square section wooden pipes which one may see in a church organ loft can be made, when necessary, in the Clevedon workshops from pine, oak or beech on the range of woodworking machinery there.

The majority of work carried out by the Company is concerned with church organs but there have been some 'domestic' organs which have had the DANIEL treatment.

There were several private organ installations in Clevedon, one as may be expected, in Mr.Daniel's house in Walton Road. This he built and expanded himself and installed it in a very elegant music room which also accommodated two grand pianos. He played the organ at All Saints Church for 50 years, so no doubt the one at home got plenty of use too. It was eventually moved to Leeds Castle in Kent.

Another was installed in Clevedon Hall/ St. Brandons and this was later moved to St. Pauls Church, Weston-s-Mare but was destroyed by enemy action when the Church was bombed on 4th January 1941.

One in a house on the corner of Sunnyside and Coleridge Road is believed to have been scrapped.

When the Curzon Picture House had a balcony and boxes, the box on the left hand side near the stage had an organ, which was removed to the United Reformed Church at Winscombe when the balcony and the boxes were closed off in the late 50's.

Mr. Caple who lived at 'Bedwyn', St. Andrews Drive had an organ built by the Company in 1960 and this was moved, in 1972, to the United Reformed Church in Nailsea. The old St Andrews Hall in Marson Road had one which went to the Masonic Hall at Six Ways.

Boddington House in Linden Road also had an organ, not a 'Daniel' but which was moved by the Company to a church in Liskeard when it was no longer required.

Back to church organs, they are now usually blown by electric motor driven bellows but a number of organs used to use a water turbine to drive the bellows. The problem was that the water usually ran to waste out of the turbine and when mains water was used and the water authorities started to put water meters in, it was found to be too expensive to run so the bellows drive was changed over to electric motor.

St. Johns Church in Clevedon was one such Church and the water turbine is still in place under the organ but is not used any more to operate the bellows of the organ.

During the war there were a number of organs rescued from bombed churches and one which found its way to Clevedon was from All Saints, Notting Hill, London. The Rev. Twisaday who knew Mr. Daniel asked him to come to London, remove the organ and store it until the Church was rebuilt after the war. The organ movement and pipes were brought to Clevedon from blitzed and burning London and were stored in Clevedon until rebuilding could take place.

Another, which was about to be installed in a church near Gloucester at the beginning of the war had parts stored in the stables of 'The Grove',the big house opposite the Old Inn and also in the red brick building where the Company first started. This building was later used as an extension workshop when the main works was full.

Organ building encompasses many skills, not least is woodworking, for the frames, pipes and of course the fine work of the keyboards and pipework surrounds. These woodworking skills were diverted during the war from organs to war-work.

The wooden patterns required for making castings for aircraft parts were produced for the Bristol Aircraft Company, and, the firm near to Daniel's at that time, Weech's Ladder Works subcontracted them to make rudders for landing craft out of massive pieces of elm.

Weech's occupied a site in the area near what was Hales Cakes and is now Clerical Medical. They were taken over by Hampton's Cabinet Makers when they moved to Clevedon after being bombed out in Bath in 1942. Hampton's had a contract for making ammunition boxes so Daniel & Co. found themselves assisting in the manufacture of these items too.

In these present times of some churches closing, Daniel & Co. still have a healthy business and, indirectly the National Lottery is helping too where churches apply for funds for overhauling their organs and the work comes to Clevedon.

Roy Girling

❑ ❑ ❑ ❑ ❑

The Antibiotic production team (Distillers Co), Clevedon 1949/50

Identification Chart (Names where known are printed on page 42)

Penicillin & Other Antibiotics

You could say that activities during the Boer War set the scene for the early production of penicillin in Clevedon!

Two of the scourges that were costing nearly twice as many lives as the fighting in the Boer War were cholera and typhoid fever and the Naval Hospital at Plymouth and later, the Royal Naval College Medical School Branch at Greenwich had the task of preparing vaccines to inoculate all fighting personnel against these diseases.

The Branch became an established part of the Navy and carried on its work down through the years when in 1938 Chief Petty Officer A. H. Lemar was in charge of the vaccine production process at the Medical School. He was given the task of preparing a continuously available one year's supply of the vaccines for all the armed forces and also of preparing a plan to be able to evacuate the laboratory to the country at two days notice in case of hostilities.

On September 2nd 1939 notice was given to evacuate the vaccine production unit of the Medical School to Barrow Gurney Hospital, Somerset, which had been taken over as a Royal Naval Auxiliary Hospital.

By September 4th all was ready, loaded up and on the move to Barrow Gurney but when they got there CPO Lemar found that the electrical, gas and water supplies were inadequate for their purposes. They looked around the district for alternative accommodation and found that the White House in Highdale Road, Clevedon was being vacated for the duration of the war by the owner, Sir Thomas Redwood.

Staff at the White House, Highdale Road

The Antibiotic Production Team (Distillers Co.) Clevedon 1949-50

1 Margaret Touke (nee Hand)
2 Pamela Blake
3 George Holland
4 Arthur Millar
5 Bert Gray
6 Mr Phillips
7 D B Kelly (Director)
8 Mr Whitmarsh
9 Gerry Milner
10 Dr Nigel E H Jones
11 Jean Saunders (nee Innes)
12 Jean Woodward-Beauman
13 May Evans (nee Turner)
14 Joan Stevens
15 Enid Bartholemew
16 Mary Willcocks (nee Hollyman)
17 Pamela Ford (nee Cook)
18 Kathleen Ballard
19 Daphne Weekes
20 Mr Clemetson (Mike's father)
21 Pamela Godfrey
22 Mr Calcot-James
23 Peggy Hedger (nee Hill)
24 Mr Mead
25 Jim Price
26 Doreen Vickery
27 Richard Codner
28 Mr Smart
29 Ron Marshall
30 Minnie Piggot
31 Pam Boyd
32 Elizabeth (Hawkins)Thompkins
33 Janet Brodie
34 Margaret Dixon
35 Hilda Sulley
36 Nancy Sulley (nee Weston)
37 Madge Hares
38 Brian Kingston
39 Margaret Snelling
40 Beryl Manley
41 E Gibson
42 Sid Brimble
43 Madeline May
44 Ann Talbot
45 Richard Holdsworth
46 Elizabeth(?) Newton
47 David Gazzard
48 Owen Hughes
49 Mr Wheeler
50 Monica Coombs
51 Mike Sheppard
52 Lawrence Jones
53
54 Johnnie O'Dwyer
55 Alan Whittaker
56 Bert Husbands
57 Robert J Pagett
58 Rosie Holland
59 Betty Brimble
60 Joan Bush
61 Kay Payne
62 Janet Lovell/Fielding
63 Trevor Cooke
64 David Locock
65 Jim Weeks
66 Bill Bonnar
67 John Cackett

40A The Cat – Buster

The house had plenty of rooms and a good cellar so it was taken over and converted into a production unit within a couple of weeks with assistance from Challicoms, Bennets, Tarr the Builders, Mr. Hurn the Gas Supply Manager, Mr. Webber the District Manager from the Electricity Board, and a representative from the Water Works - Mr. Fry?

Two boys were required for messenger duties and the science teacher, Mr.Kitchen at the local school was approached to recommend two likely lads. Peter Norris and ? Livesey were selected and they trained as technicians in addition to their messenger duties and eventually joined the Navy when they were 18.

The Commanding Officer was Captain Ashcroft assisted by Surgeon Commander Hitch together with Commander Green (see Photograph). George Russell, the recently retired Clevedon Postmaster, was a telegraph boy at the time and well remembers delivering telegrams to Captain Ashcroft!

When production was well under way the Admiralty ordered that anti-tetanus be added to the typhoid/cholera vaccine and this required the obtaining of tetanus toxoid cultures in order to start off the growth of the necessary foundation for the vaccine. The problem was where to get these cultures.

The Naval Medical School provided accommodation for Medical Research Council staff and a young graduate pathologist who was seconded to the vaccine production group also came to The White House in Clevedon.

The graduate knew where to get tetanus toxoid, from Dr. Fleming at St. Mary's Hospital in London. So with CPO Lemar a visit was made to see Dr. Fleming who confirmed that he could supply their needs. While they were at the hospital he showed them his experiments with his discovery of the mould which had powerful bacteria killing capability which he called penicillin from the name of the mould penicillium notatum.

Dr. Fleming gave them a sample of his penicillin culture along with the tetanus toxoid and when they got back to Clevedon the pathologist took the penicillin and started to experiment with the extraction of the active principle. The result was a brew which looked like scrumpy according to Mr. Lemar.

With advice from other bodies who were also experimenting with penicillin they were able to produce some with enough concentration to send to Barrow Gurney Hospital to put on the wounds of patients there to see the effect. In those days there was no drugs approval process to go through so it was fairly straight forward to do some human guinea pig testing. Wounds which had been festering for months cleared up in two or three days.

This gave encouragement to extend the production to make enough to send to each of the Naval Hospitals at Chatham, Portsmouth and Plymouth where again it was used on wounds and also venereal disease sores which cleared up in a matter of days instead of the two or three months it had been taking in hospital.

A visit by Naval Top Brass to Clevedon to see the source of this miracle resulted in a report to The First Lord of the Admiralty, Mr. A. V. Alexander (who incidentally was born at No.33 George Street W-s-M). He in turn told the Prime Minister, Winston Churchill who then ordered that production should be increased and whatever facilities needed should be provided.

The White House was not large enough to cope with any increase in capacity so CPO Lemar went looking around the town for possible larger premises and met Captain D.L.Reece who was headmaster at Clevedon College, a boys' school which was just in the process of closing down. After a look at the school, which was situated at No. 5 Elton Road, the Navy decided to requisition the building and everything was transferred there from the White House. (The White House then became a MoF base for the area)

No. 5 Elton Road became the base for three separate lines of activity, one, the production of T A B vaccine and Tetanus Toxoid for the Royal Navy, two, the training of Laboratory Sick Berth Staff for their Hygiene Course to allow them to be granted Laboratory Status in the Navy, and three, and by far the most important, the production of penicillin for the Royal Navy and the other Armed Services.

The large double fronted Victorian building was very good and adequate in size for initial research but too small for the large scale production of penicillin.

In the rear of the house there was a large garden and in this, in 1944 the erection (by Carrier & Co.of Sussex) of a building took place to house the required facilities.

Two large Incubator Rooms housed hundreds of milk bottles on mobile racks which were moved around to enable the mould to be harvested.

Each of the bottles held a culture medium based on brewery washings and into this was injected a suspension of the mould using a paint spray gun. This work was carried out by Voluntary Aid Detachment (VAD) and local girls.

After a period of about ten days, a mat of mould had developed on top of the culture fluid and the the bottles were carried, by overhead machinery to a collecting point where they were vigorously shaken and emptied, the fluid being then transferred to the Plant Room. The empty bottles were washed, sterilised, refilled with culture medium and mould and returned to the incubator room to start the process over again. The air in the incubators was continuously washed and sterilised to avoid contamination and the temperature maintained at 22 degrees C, the optimum temperature for the mould to grow.

In the Plant Room the fluid, which contained a low level of penicillin, went through a process of extraction and concentration, the resulting output then being placed in small bottles and loaded into a freeze drying plant. This reduced the fluid to a fine powder and each bottle was sealed, labelled with date, batch number and directions for reconstitution with sterile water. Boxes were packed with several bottles each and despatched to Royal Naval Hospitals and other grateful recipients.

This 'factory' was managed by Petty Officer J. A. Roberts who had been at the White House for six months in 1939/40 and who returned to Clevedon soon after D-Day in 1944. During the whole of the manufacturing process an Assay Laboratory was responsible for measuring amounts of penicillin present at each stage of production. The Assay Laboratory was staffed by R.N. personnel, VAD's and ladies recruited locally.

The organisation and some of the staff names which have been remembered are shown below:

Royal Naval Medical School- No.5 Elton Road - Clevedon

Senior Naval Staff

Surgeon Captains Ashcroft, Hitch and W. Mussen
Commander C.A. Green and Surgeon Commander W.S.Millar

Civilian Research Scientists
D.L.Johnson
F(?)Kitchen

R.N. Regulation Staff
Warrant Officer Lemar
CPOs Waller & Donaldson

Pathology ? Gley — ***Serology*** ? Gill

Penicillin Plant & Production
Cmdr Green
P.O.'s J.A.Roberts & C.A.Reading

Media Autoclaving Sterilizing
Various Local Civilian Staff

Mycology Culture Inoculation
P.O.Tailby

Extraction Purification Vacuum Drying
P.O.Couzens

Assay
V.A.D. Detachment

Civilian Ward Staff

Hygiene -? Fredericks
-? Cook
Bacteriology -? Freshfield
-? Webb
Animal Colony -? Waltham
Administration Hazel ?.

Local Civilian Staff Miss J. Hedges, Miss P. Hedges, Miss ? Skinner, Miss P. Neath, Miss J. Brimble

Tetanus Vaccine Growth
P.O. G.Lane
S/B P.O. J.Lineham
S/B P.O. G.Kneale
also responsible for freeze drying plant.

The whole establishment at 5 Elton Road took part in the Standardisation of Penicillin in conjunction with other laboratories in the U.K. and the U.S.A.

It is very pleasing to note that some of the vital early days of penicillin research and production in the U.K. took place in Clevedon, using local facilities and members of the local population to support the R.N. staff. The penicillin was distributed to all the Armed Services and was particularly effective in saving many lives during the invasion of Europe after D-Day.

In a report in the Clevedon Mercury of May 25th 1946, Captain Mussen said that now penicillin was being produced in large quantities in purpose built factories the small scale production in Clevedon was no longer viable and would be closed down.

The Distillers Company bought No.5 Elton Road from the Navy and continued producing some penicillin there. However the demand for penicillin became so great that the Distillers Company put in hand the development of a mass production process at their plant at High Wycombe and production was enventually transferred to that site. It is interesting to note that our President and History Group Chairman, George Case was a member of the team which developed the penicillin production process machinery for a similar plant in I.C.I.

Elton Road was then taken over in 1949 by the Medical Research Council and the staff continued in the development of new antibiotics. Around about this time the staff numbered between 60 & 70 and the photograph shows them on the steps of No 5 Elton Road around 1949/50. Some of the people in the photograph still live in and around the district and from them many of the names have been remembered.

Attention was being given to bacteria that were resistant to penicillin and samples of strains of bacteria and fungi from various countries were sent to Clevedon. One organism, isolated from a sewage outfall in Sardinia, was developed in Clevedon into the nucleus of an alternative antibiotic called CEPHALOSPORIN from which a wide range of products have been manufactured all over the world, one of them having the trade name of CEPOREX.

In the efforts to improve the yield of anti-biotics from the fermentation process, the Elton Road Group was one of the first comparatively large scale users in this country of synthetic ion exchange resins. Culture fermentation was managed by Ron Harrison who worked there from 1954/5 to 1960 and then returned to university to become a dentist in which capacity he has served Clevedon until his recent retirement.

Continuous production of antibiotics was carried on in Clevedon until the early 1960's when work was transferred to Porton Down when the work there on biological warfare was wound down.

No.5 Elton Road is now split up into offices and, possibly, the people who occupy them now have little idea of the lives that have been saved by the work that went on there in the past.

Roy Girling

❑ ❑ ❑ ❑ ❑

Two Timber Merchants

The Shopland Sawmills

Now into the fourth generation the Company was established in Clevedon in 1862 by the Great Grandfather of the present owner Councillor D. W. Shopland.

Great Grandfather William and his brothers moved to Clevedon from Cullompton in Devon and between them set up not only the sawmill but also a brickworks with housing for their work people. It is reckoned that as a family they built about one third of Victorian Clevedon. The brickworks was sold, in 1898, with all its equipment and goodwill to Sidney Keen who owned the Strode Road Brickworks and Pottery.

Many of the very decorative barge boards seen on the houses all over Clevedon were made by hand at the saw mills using a band saw and jigs to produce a variety of designs which are probably unique to the town.

William's son, E. H. Shopland started work at his father's brick works in Kenn Road, and later, at the age of 19, drove the Council's steam roller. He was also a very skillful black- smith producing ironwork for many applications around the town and surrounding areas. He left the shoeing of horses to the other four blacksmiths in the town and his forge and chimney with its decorated top is still to be seen by the sawmill in Old Street.

The Mileage Yard on 8th April 1964

At 24, after marriage, he bought a traction engine and trailer to haul lime from Clevedon to Bristol and coke breeze on the return journey. Problems with the law - speeding at 4 mph through the local villages - and with local opposition caused him to sell out. Later he bought a small traction engine to restart the haulage business then sold this engine to buy a bigger one followed by a road locomotive which he named "Clevedonia". This was used a couple of times to take the Methodist Sunday School Annual Picnic 6 miles to Naish House at the top of Wraxall Hill towing three trailers.

Mr. E. H. Shopland was a Methodist Local Preacher and as such had to visit churches all over the area which he did on his bicycle. On one occasion, when he had an appointment at Portishead Methodist Church he found he had a puncture in his bicycle tyre. Mr. R. Stephens ran a bicycle shop as well as his motor car factory in the Triangle so he went there for help and Mr. Stephens said " I will run you there in my car". Going was a speedy journey in daylight but the return journey in the dark was a different matter because the only light they had was a candle in a jam jar!!

This was in 1897 and at that time Mr. Stephens was designing and building cars and eventually ran a local passenger service with them. Shopland's provided a lot of the original body work frames and the wooden pulleys for the variable speed transmission system.

After the death of his father Mr. Shopland restarted the sawmill business with a portable steam engine which had been used to drive the mortar mill during the building of the new Clevedon Methodist Church. This engine was eventually replaced by a horizontal steam engine complete with boiler obtained from the first Clevedon Water Company building (which was on the site of the present fire station) when it was superseded by the new pumping station built in 1902 in Tickenham Road. This engine answered the purpose splendidly for many years.

In 1915 during the First World War a number of Portugese soldiers were drafted to Britain to assist in the war effort and 30 or 40 of these came to Clevedon and were billeted in the sawmill building. In 1918 when they were due to return to Portugal there was some difficulty in them taking home the money they had earned. By borrowing a 5/8th's inch drill from the mill they each drilled holes in the heels of their boots and packed away sovereigns then nailed an extra piece of leather over the top. As far as is known they got out of Britain and back into Portugal with the money undetected.

After the First World War ended there was need for expansion and as steam power was still the favourite, Mr. E. H. Shopland decided to buy a one hundred and fifty horse power engine from a firm in Newcastle under Lyme, it had a 7 ton flywheel, 12 feet in diameter and served the company until motive power was changed over to electric motor. The boiler house chimney has remained though, as a memorial to the good old days of steam!

The Company has been in business now for 135 years in Clevedon and the last one hundred years has seen an uninterrupted period of operation on the present site in Old Street. It is still providing timber for many applications to locations all over Somerset and beyond.

William Staddon & Son Ltd.

Clevedon must always have had a very good reputation when you consider the number of people who seemingly out of the blue decided to make their homes and businesses here. William Staddon is another fine example, he came, in 1920, from a good job at Knights in London to set up his timber yard in part of the Clevedon Station Yard which he rented from the GWR. His office can be seen, partially hidden by the crane in the photograph and is around about where the pet supplies shop is now, opposite Frank's Audio Visual Company. The business is still thriving under the management of his great-grandson Ian in The Barn in Parnell Road.

William was born in Bristol in 1880 and started work in January 1895 at Messrs Grace & Hayes Timber Merchants at Broad Weir Bristol at 4 shillings/week (20p).

Mr William Staddon at the door of his office in Clevedon GWR Station Yard

Later, in 1895 he started wood carving as a hobby and this together with walking and cycling around the district, his spare time seems to have been fully occupied. In his diaries written between 1882 & 1908 he mentions making a number of visits to Clevedon, by boat and train from Bristol, by bike and by walking the Portishead to Clevedon coast path so perhaps he had the town in the back of his mind for many years as a possible place to live and work.

He was very interested in hardwoods and arranged for the native species of ash and oak logs to be delivered, by rail, from Honiton into the siding at Clevedon.

The logs were unloaded using the hand operated 8 ton crane which was mounted in the siding. What a tiring job it must have been to wind the grab up and down the number of times it took to promptly unload and stack the piles of logs which had arrived so that the rail trucks could be cleared from the siding to allow others to be shunted in. The timber was left to season naturally in the yard until it was ready for use.

In the early days of the business the sawmill was not able to cope with some of the larger logs so these were transported down the road to Mr E.H.Shoplands yard to be cut up on the big engine driven saw.

William's son William Clifford was born in September 1908 and joined his father in the business in 1923 continuing the interest in hardwoods. When William Clifford's son John joined the business in 1951 he branched out into softwoods which were in great demand for all the house building which was taking place. John's son Ian joined him in 1986 to carry on the business after he retired in 1992. Now Ian has extended the range to include imported hardwoods and softwoods and he and his staff are able to meet a demand for many shapes and sizes of timber for both the domestic and business community using the range of cutting and shaping machinery they have installed in The Barn.

Before Staddons took over the Barn it had been used by a company for building coaches, ambulances and similar vehicles, so there must be another story waiting to be told on that activity.

Roy Girling

❑ ❑ ❑ ❑ ❑

The Utilities - Water, Gas & Electricity

Water

A major factor in deciding on a place to found a settlement was the presence of a water supply and the springs coming out of the limestone hills around the area we know as Clevedon no doubt had an influence on there being people settled here from pre-historic times.

Before the middle of the 1800's most of Clevedon's population lived at or below the spring level because building on the higher levels was restricted by the inability to store water in the permeable limestone. The health of the residents of these lower levels of Clevedon suffered greatly from water borne diseases brought about by pollution of the water sources. These were in general the streams and rhynes fed by the springs and, as they acted as drains and sewers too it wasn't surprising that the mortality rate, especially in children was very high.

In 1865 The Clevedon Waterworks Company was founded following the sinking of a borehole in 1864. A reservoir was built on Dial Hill, fed by a new steam driven pump over the borehole which was sited in Old Street where the Fire Station is now. The Engineers responsible for the work were Lawson & Mansergh of London, the contractor was W. Green of Clevedon and the pumping engine came from Stothert & Pitt. From this time onwards, health improved, building went ahead on the hills and Clevedon began to grow. A report in a Guide Book of 1879 recorded that professional analysis

Pumping Station *Michael Horsfield*

pronounced Clevedon water to be exceedingly pure and fit for all purposes. In fact by about 1890 Clevedon's death rate was less than half that of the average for the whole country. Water was supplied at first by a network of about seven miles of pipes but was continually being extended to meet the town's growth which, towards the end of the 1800's meant that the demand for water was outstripping the available supply and this was becoming too salty to use. The Waterworks Company therefore decided on a completely new development and in 1902 opened the pumping station on Tickenham Road.

The pumping station building is a splendid example of solid Victorian architecture and was purpose built to last. It is embellished with some fine ornate stone work created in the days when architectural excellence was important and money no object! The Clevedon Waterworks Company was taken over by the Bristol Waterworks Company in 1953 but the old Coat of Arms is still to be seen on the lintel over the front door.

A first well was sunk, down to a depth of 110 feet and then extended, in 1914, with a borehole down to 267 feet. The original pump was driven by a Glenfield & Kennedy vertical compound steam engine, the pump having a capacity of 720,000 gallons per day (GPD). This was a smaller version of the beam engines which can be seen, now retained as museum pieces at the Blagdon Pumping Station.

In 1916 a Marshal horizontal compound engine was installed and this was followed, in 1938 by a steam turbine driving a centrifugal pump of 144,000 G.P.D. capacity. For reasons of efficiency the steam driven pumps were later replaced by electric submersible well pumps fed from the mains with an emergency stand-by generator supply and this is how the pumping station operates at the present time. The landmark chimney tower, although no longer used, has been retained and preserved as a feature of the site.

About half of Clevedon's water comes from the well and borehole under the pumping station with the remainder coming from Chelvey. Water treatment, softening and chlorination is carried out on site before the water is pumped up to the reservoirs on Dial Hill from whence it is distributed around the town.

The Gas Works

The Clevedon Gas Company established a gas works in 1857 on a site in Parnell Road and in 1862 there was local canvassing for support for the introduction of public lighting, by gas, around the town. This proposal appeared to have a mixed reception and so was put to the vote. This resulted in 115 for; 63 against and 66 neutral.

On the basis of this result The Clevedon Gas Company undertook to supply, light and maintain a system of street lighting, the first lamp being lit in 1863. In order to economise, the lamps were not lit at times of full moon nor during June and July but one can imagine the dramatic change that illuminated streets must have made to life of the town, especially in wintertime. Gas lighting continued and spread with the growth of the town until the changeover to electric lighting in the 1930's.

When Electricity came to Clevedon

The Clevedon Mercury reported on 26th September 1903 that there was a serious proposal to introduce electric light to Clevedon from the Weston super Mare and District Electric Supply Company Ltd. The Company was to investigate whether it would prove to be a profitable speculation but as no further developments appear to have taken place on this proposal, it can only be assumed that the likely return on the necessary investment was considered inadequate. Clevedon had to rely on gas for another 20 years before getting its own electricity supply.

In 1911 The Clevedon and District/North Somerset Electricity Co.Ltd. was formed and a minute book established, and from this book we find that the Company was set up by Christy Brothers of Chelmsford.

Mr. Frank Christy was an active member of the small Board of Directors (which included Mr. Woodington from the Boot Factory) when they established generating facilities at Gas Lane (now Old Mill Road)in Portishead. The building is still in existence (1996). The small engine driven unit generated d.c. power and the Company had the intention of building a similar unit in Clevedon but this never came to pass.

Towards the end of the First World War, the War Ministry paid for a high voltage (11,000 Volt) a.c. cable to be laid from Bower Ashton (Bristol City Electricity Dept) to Portishead for a port facility at Portbury but the war ended before it could be built. The cable must have been little used for some time because it wasn't until 22nd July 1921 that it was used supply Portishead when they changed over from the dc generator to ac power from Bristol.

But what about Clevedon? Well, it is recorded that the first talks about extending the cable to Clevedon from Portishead were held on 16th December 1921 after applications had been received from Clevedon and Nailsea residents who wanted to have this new fangled stuff in their homes, just like Portishead. On February 11th 1922 the Board had a meeting to decide on the acceptance of a quotation from Henley's Cables Ltd for the high voltage cable extension. Substation sites were approved for acquisition at Long Ashton, Flax Bourton, Wraxall and Nailsea on 12th July 1922.

Almost another year passed when on June 7th 1923, a public meeting was held in Clevedon "to ascertain the amount of support likely to be forthcoming". The results must have been favourable because by June 14th 1923, only one week later, a substation site had been acquired in East Clevedon. Work went ahead at great speed and by Autumn 1923 Clevedon, and Nailsea had an electricity supply available.

It was further reported on 7th May 1924 that electricity showrooms and dwellings connected up to the new supply were in existence in both Clevedon and Nailsea. Local companies were well to the fore in offering their services to install cables and outlets for power and light in homes and businesses. Now if we get that rare event, an interruption in supply, pretty well everything stops and it causes us to wonder how we ever got on without that invisible but so essential service.

Roy Girling

Willcocks' workshop, Old Church Road - G. A. Willcocks and son Gilbert

Jack Willcocks with Leslie Halliwell and Sir Henry Seagrave moments before disaster

Willcocks Engineering Co.

The Willcocks family came to Clevedon from Haverhill in Suffolk in 1883 and opened their first shop, making bicycles, in Lime Kiln Lane. They moved from there to Queens Road to the building where the motor accessory shop Top Gear is now situated, and finally to the corner of Old Church Road and Pizey Avenue where they are today. Their first workshop on this site is shown here with father, George Alexander Willcocks standing on the left and second son, Gilbert at work on a lathe.

There were three brothers and each had his own interest, Harry, the eldest, was an engineer but he also undertook the administration of the Company. The second brother Gilbert was a toolmaker, having served his apprenticeship with White & Poppies of Coventry, and Michael, or Jack, as he was known was the precision engineering specialist.

Jack was a member of the crew of three when Sir Henry Seagrave made his bid to break the water speed record in 1930 on Lake Windermere in his speedboat "Miss England II". The attempt ended in disaster on June 13th 1930 and Jack was the only survivor. The photograph opposite shows the boat moments before it sank and below is a photograph of the crew - Leslie Halliwell of Portishead on the left, Sir Henry Seagrave having his life jacket fastened and Jack Willcocks of Clevedon on the right.

The crew of Miss England II - Willcocks is seen on the right

The Blue Ensign from the boat was retrieved from the lake and now resides in the Clubhouse at the Clevedon Sailing Club, while the windscreen and Seagrave's seat are in the Museum in Windermere, having been taken there by Aubrey Willcocks, Jack's nephew.

Donald Campbell, in the preparation for his record breaking runs in his boat 'Bluebird', invited Jack to Lake Coniston to look over the boat to give the benefit of his experience.

When Willcock's Garage was opened in 1927/28, the Company introduced the first charabanc to Clevedon and they had some of the early cars available for hire. In the photo is a Hampton 11.9 and behind it a Napier with a tip-up body. The latter was used to transport stone from excavations at Clevedon Hall across the road to fill in and build up the ground around the garage. On the left of the picture can be seen the start of the building for the garage workshops.

The engineering company which was set up by Jack in the late 30's comprised 20 employees who had come from BAC and one of their first jobs was, as might be expected, of a racing nature. On the corner of Pizey Avenue there was a car race track which hadn't been used for some time and the associated racing cars were in a somewhat derelict condition but out of them all they made four or five serviceable units which they were able to use on the track. The photograph shows the setup in operation.

I wonder if there were any comments from the neighbours !?

Willcocks' Garage

Brooklands Miniature Car Track. - Wilcocks (Clevedon) Ltd.

When the war started in 1939, the Company became engaged in making jigs and tools for use by the armaments factory at Woolwich and this firmly established them as a precision engineering Company and resulted in a wide range of jobs requiring individual and inventive expertise. One item of particular interest was an early type of digital counter in the form of a disc perforated with a pattern of holes. When fixed to a drive shaft it could be scanned with a lamp and detector to give a readout of direction and degree of movement of the shaft. Typical uses were on gun mountings to correlate with a direction finder and on the gyro-compass on aircraft automatic pilot equipment to maintain a given bearing. These and many other similar applications were of vital importance in helping to maintain a state of one-upmanship over the enemy.

Before the days of the electron microscope, magnifcation depended upon systems of lens' and mirrors and in order to achieve high levels of magnification a very high accuracy of grinding and polishing of the optics was necessary. One of the scientists engaged in microscope development, Dr. Burch, introduced Willcock's Company to the techniques of optical component manufacture and they soon became specialists in the field. One of the designs they manufactured, for cancer research, was Dr. Burch's reflecting microscope, which gave a fixed magnification of 10,000 times, one of the highest levels reached until the electron microscope.

In the early 1950's Jack's son Christopher contracted polio myelitis, or infantile paralysis as it used to be called, and was taken to Ham Green Hospital under the care of Dr. James Macrae. An essential item in the care and treatment of polio was the "iron lung" which provided the necessary effort to expand and contract the patient's chest when the body's own muscle power was disabled by the disease.

On visiting his son in the Hospital he found that the iron lung was a large piece of equipment installed in the hospital and available only to a patient who had been brought there in time.

Jack Willcocks studied the design of the machine and, after a discussion about its application and use with the Staff at Ham Green, came back to the workshops in Clevedon and set about designing a more portable and automatic unit which could be made readily available to sufferers who were unable to get to a hospital equipped with an iron lung.

The development was sucessful and the Company went on to make several units which were used all over the country and abroad during that period in the 50s when the disease struck down many, mainly young, people before the Salk and later vaccines were developed for immunisation against the virus. The 'Clevedon Respirator' was the subject of an article in The Lancet of November 1953 in which it was described how one patient's life had been saved by being put onto the respirator after failing to respond to treatment in the traditional 'iron lung'. A photograph from the front cover of the Willcocks Company's description of the respirator is shown.

Another precision instrument they made for the medical fraternity was the microtome, a device for making very thin slices of a pathology sample for viewing under a microscope for diagnostic purposes.

Later on in the 1950s a request came for the Company to design and fabricate balloons for high-altitude weather research. This necessitated building a hut with a controlled atmosphere and having a 100 ft. long table on which to lay out the panels of polythene from which the balloons were made. A seam welding machine was made to roll along the table on guide rails to weld the panels together to make balloons as long as 300 ft. and 120 ft. diameter.

This work went on for about 10 years and the balloons were released from the old airship base at Cardington, in India and in Australia. The picture shows one being prepared for take off. The test equipment to be carried by the balloons was installed

The Clevedon Positive Pressure Respirator

in aluminium spheres made in two halves and bolted together. Some of the larger ones measured as much as 10 feet in diameter and when any of the balloons were released into the atmosphere they had details on them of whom to contact when the balloon and its instrument sphere came down to earth. On one occasion ,in India, attempts were made to find a balloon which was thought to have descended in a particular area but local residents professed complete ignorance of any such event. However on making a further search around, a local inhabitant was found bathing in a large semispherical aluminium bath which he insisted had been in his family for generations! After some persuasion he revealed where the other half of the sphere and the test equipment were hidden!

A tall building was added to the end of the balloon shop to house a press to fabricate helicopter rotor blades from carbon fibre, these having been designed by a Willcocks nephew, Ronald Clemens, making another 'first' for Clevedon.

Another problem which Willcocks Co. solved in the mid 60's was that of preventing unscrupulous bar tenders from topping up their bottles of spirits with water. They invented a non-reversible bottle top which when crimped onto the bottle by the distillers, allowed the contents to be poured out but prevented anything, like water, from being poured in so maintaining the strength of the brew!

Weather Balloon

When, in the late 60's, the variety of car engines required 2,3 or 4 star petrol, Willcocks were asked if they could design a blending pump which would allow the use of one nozzle to dispense the desired blend. In the final design, installed at a garage near Windsor, the pump was on an island and the nozzle could be moved round into any of three positions so a car could pull up into an empty space on the island and swing the nozzle round, select the blend and fill up. The next customer, having pulled into another space on the island would swing the pipe to his car and select his blend without having to wait for the previous car to move away. The idea failed because of suspicion by customers as to whether the right blend was being supplied by the one pipe, so the old system continues of a pump and pipe for each different blend.

The Company has been called upon many times to assist with various problems of design and manufacture but perhaps one of the strangest calls for assistance was to house two elephants when the circus 'big top' erected on Salthouse Fields was damaged during a storm in 1954/55. Straw was strewn around in the garage and the elephants are seen to have settled down quite well. Not so was Jack's son Christopher who was out with friends when the animals had been brought in. When he arrived home later after a convivial evening and opened the door to drive in he wondered if he had been too covivial, it was only the fact that the elephants were grey, not pink, that he felt somewhat reassured.

In 1964 a call for engineering assistance came from Sergeant John Durston of the Clevedon Police Force when a schoolboy reported that a flying saucer had landed on Dial Hill! Aubrey Willcocks and Reg Woollard went to investigate and on trying to move the object to find an opening, the 'saucer' started bleeping. They waited to see if any little green men emerged but nothing further happened so they set about opening it up. Inside they found an Exide battery, a loudspeaker and a switch which operated a bleeper when the 'saucer' was moved. Reg Woollard commented that all the parts were made

Elephants from Salthouse Fields 1954/55

in Britain, not Mars, and the liquid which filled the lower part of the fibreglass body was found to be pig-swill!

This was one of five similar objects found on that day in various parts of the country, all part of a great practical joke by members of an apprentice training school 'somewhere in England'. In the picture Sergeant Durston looks on while Reg Woollard attacks the switch and Aubrey Willcocks holds the battery and loudspeaker.

Willcocks Engineering Co. have now been part of the Clevedon scene for over 110 years and staff from the Company have gone on to found further engineering companies in the town (of which more in the future) so it is likely that similar work will go on well into the next century.

Roy Girling

Flying Saucer?

POSSIBLE CHAPTERS FOR A FUTURE BOOK

The collecting together of the information on the Industrial History of the Town has been a most fascinating exercise with one main problem - where to draw the line and get on with having it printed.

Every topic researched has revealed information on yet another aspect of industrial activity in Clevedon so it is very likely that there will be many comments from readers on what hasn't been included.

However there is always the opportunity of putting together another book and the following list gives some idea of the topics which might be included. Therefore, if you have further information, photographs or anecdotes of the subects covered here, the proposed future ones, or of ones we have left out or didn't know about then The Civic Society Local History Group would be very pleased to hear from you.

AERATED WATER PRODUCTION

AIRCRAFT DESIGN:
- BAC
- FOLLANDS

BASKET MAKING

BLACKSMITHS

CAKE FACTORY

COAL IMPORT WHARF

DAIRIES

ENGINEERING COMPANIES:
- AMPEP
- AIM (Automatic Industrial Machines)
- 'ENGINEERS BLUE'

FISHING

QUARRYING

SALT PANNING

❑ ❑ ❑ ❑ ❑

PART TWO
MORE SOCIAL HISTORY

Note: Refer to the earlier books published by the Society for other aspects of Clevedon's growth through the ages.

FROM VILLAGE TO TOWN	1981
THE ANNALS OF CLEVEDON	1988
CLEVEDON PAST	1993

A Hill Far Away

In the churchyard of our old church of St. Andrews, close to the entrance stands a gravestone which reads:-

"In affectionate remembrance of Caroline Wreford youngest and much beloved daughter of William and Caroline Durbin"

Below are the the words which are unusual for an English gravestone.

"Also of Frederick oldest and much beloved son of the above (He fell in the battle of Gettysburg, Pennsylvania) July 1863 aged 22 years."

As a Clevedonian and member of the History Group of the local Civic Society, I became interested and although we shall probably never know why this young man left Clevedon to travel to America and join the army, an opportunity arose to fill some gaps.

This opportunity arose because some years ago when living in Highdale Avenue an American family moved in next door. As a result of the friendship which grew between us, we were invited to visit them in the States when they returned home.

This we did seven years ago when we travelled from their home in Illinois to Colorado with them. When deciding to visit again we thought we would like to see some of the eastern USA, so we planned to fly to Washington, hire a car and drive to Illinois.

It was then when studying the map we thought , as Gettysburg was only 78 miles from Washington, why not visit the battle site, now a national memorial park.

This we did, armed with information from the History Group who had written and obtained service records stating that "Sergeant Fred Durbin 1st Company, 78th Infantry Regiment, 3rd Brigade 2nd Division,XII Corp" was killed on July 2nd 1863 and first buried on the north side of Spanglers field, later reburied in the

Durbin was a sergeant by the time of the battle of Gettysburg.

memorial graveyard. With the help of a Warden at the park centre we located his grave and paid our respects.

But why Gettysburg should be the site for the decisive battle of the American Civil War requires an understanding of the situation in 1863.

To explain the reasons for the war would take too long, they are complicated so we will pass to the military strategy. Although America is a very large country the capitals of the opposing states were only one hundred miles apart. That of the Union at Washington on the northern border of Virginia and that of the Confederacy at Richmond, central Virginia. By 1863 a number of battles had been fought over northern Virginia, like a grim game of chess each army trying to capture the capital of the opposing side.

By 1863 the Confederate Army, although winning battles under the clever leadership of its Commander, General Robert E Lee, was becoming weaker without the manpower and industrial might that the north possessed.

The Union Army, although the stronger, was dogged by a succession of weak commanding Generals, starting with McClellan who fancied himself as a new Napoleon, but was not; he was replaced by Burnside who gave his name to sideburns because of his excessive whiskers; he was followed by Hooker who is remembered in America because he closed down the Army brothels and in revenge the soldiers christened the occupants of such places "Hookers". Hooker was replaced just before Gettysburg by Meade, who was fussy but efficient.

The only really successful Union Commander was a scruffy little hard drinking man named Ulysses S Grant, at this time besieging the last confederate fort on the Mississippi, one thousand miles to the west of Vicksburg.

What kind of a war was it? It had started with outdated tactics based on previous wars when the main infantry weapon was the muzzle loading smoothbore musket. It was possible to make mass attacks against defended positions as the musket was only effective at some one hundred yards.

Although the musket used in the Civil War was still muzzle-loading it was rifled. Previous difficulty of loading a rifled musket, namely forcing the ball down the muzzle had been made easy by the invention of the minie ball. A conical bullet with a hollow base which when fired expanded to fill the grooves of the rifling. The effective range had risen to over five hundred yards and accuracy vastly improved, therefore casualties were high. The soft lead bullets caused terrible wounds noticeably to limbs where the only hope was amputation before gangrene set in. Hygiene was none existent and of the total during this war of 600,000 dead, nearly half would die of illnesses caused by wounds or diseases such as Cholera, Typhoid, Scarlet Fever, measles and others - today dealt with easily by antibiotics.

The loading of the musket was a slow job. It was first necessary to extract a paper cartridge (thus cartridge paper, still used) from an ammunition pouch; bite off the end and hold the bullet in the mouth, pour the powder down the muzzle, split the

bullet in, right way up, place the paper on top and ram the lot down the barrel with a rammer carried in a tube under the barrel then replace the rammer. Pull back the hammer at the breech, reach for a cap (like those used today in children's guns), place it over a hollow stud protruding from the breech, aim and fire. Repeat the whole procedure about four times a minute. The powder was black powder and blackened the hands and faces - on a still day a fog hung over the battlefield.

Many of the rifles were Enfield rifles manufactured in England and sold to both sides, as were some of the advanced cannons manufactured by Whitworth. By the end of the war the invention of the copper or brass cartridge case had produced reliable breech loading guns and even repeaters.

After the battle of Gettysburg the northern war office collected all discarded muskets and found that twenty per cent had been incorrectly loaded with several cartridges because in the heat of battle soldiers had forgotten to cap the gun. It forced the US Army to convert after the war, to breech loading weapons. A Bayonet could be attached to the muzzle when required. We still today fix our electric light bulbs in the same manner. We call it a Bayonet catch.

The uniforms of dark blue for the Union Troops and grey for the Confederates need little description, we have all seen "Gone with the Wind" or similar films which portray them admirably; although like most Hollywood films, the uniforms are too clean and tidy. By 1863 shortage of grey cloth in the south resulted in many of their soldiers being dressed in home spun uniforms dyed brown. They also lacked shoes - more of that later.

During the early part of 1863, heavy fighting took place in the centre of Virginia near Richmond. A stalemate was reached where the two armies faced each other across the Rappahonnoch river, both recovering from heavy casualties.

A plan was conceived by the southern High Command to relieve the pressure on Richmond, that Lee's Army would carry out a flanking move, back into the west, and in the cover of Shenandoah Valley move north around the Union Army into Maryland and Pennsylvania, thus threatening to cut off Washington, and by invading the north, force the Union to the negotiation table.

The movement took place, but a problem arose. For the first time Lee was badly let down by his Cavalry under its leader General Stuart. JEB Stuart was a flamboyant character, a hero in the south with a following like a pop star today. He wore beautifully fitted uniforms complete with a wide brimmed hat with a black ostrich feather attached. He took with him on his staff a banjo player to entertain around the campfire.

Instead of watching the northern Army and informing Lee of their position he decided to go off on a harassing raid and disappeared almost altogether from the campaign. Lee did not know where the Union Army was, the latter in their turn followed a parallel course north with only a rough idea of where Lee was.

So we arrive at the first day of July when the Confederate Army had penetrated the northern state of Pennsylvania and, at the northern end of the Blue Ridge Mountains, was some ten miles to the west of Gettysburg. The General commanding the lead division heard that there was a warehouse full of boots in Gettysburg of which his Army was desperately short, so swung his division east.

At the same time the advanced Cavalry scouting ahead of the Union Army had entered the town and passed through when they clashed with advancing Confederates. They dismounted and opened fire, at the same time sending urgent messages to the main Union Army to hurry up and join them. Thus almost by accident began the three day decisive battle of Gettysburg.

A brief description of the ground; it was mostly open farmland with low ridges and hills, some wooded. The main features are to the north and on the southern edge of the town are two hills joined by a saddle; the one crowned by the town cemetery and called Cemetery Hill the other Culps Hill. Some two miles south are two small conical hills, Round Top and Little Round Top joined to the northern hills by a ridge dipping in the centre. Ease of Culps Hill a meadow runs down to a small stream, this is Spangler's Field and will feature in our narrative. To the west beyond a shallow valley, running north to south lies a wooded ridge with a seminary at its northern end, thus Seminary Ridge.

To return to the days of action, the outnumbered union Cavalry Scouts fell back on the town and retreated through it to form a defensive position on Cemetery Hill and the high ground. There they held, and with nightfall the battle fizzled out. All night both sides reinforced their positions.

Northern Troops arriving in the bright moonlight would have just been able to read a notice on the cemetery gate stating

"There will be a fine of five dollars for anyone discharging a firearm within the cemetery."

The second day commenced with attacks on the left flank of the Union Army and spread into heavy fighting to decide who should occupy the Round Top Hills. It was only just won by the Union Army - failure would have rendered their whole position untenable. Later in the evening a corp of Confederate Infantry attacked Union positions on Culps Hill, it failed, but not before the defenders had lost ground on their right flank at Spanglers field. We will return to this action.

Finally, on the third day after a huge artillery bombardment, at midday the Confederate Army, launched an all-out attack by some twelve thousand men against the centre of the Union Army facing Seminary Ridge. It failed with terrible casualties. This attack (known as Picketts Charge after the Commander of this Division) had just reached a stone wall where a memorial stands today inscribed with the words "High Water Mark." It was not only the high water mark of the Confederate attack, but of the whole war - after this, the South could only retreat on all fronts. Although the war would drag on for another year or so the outcome was decided here.

The Armies paused on the fourth day, no action took place. Then Lee's Army retreated back across the Potomac river into Virginia - also on the fourth of July. Far away in the west Vicksburg surrendered. The south was split in two. Incidentally, until quite recently Vicksburg did not celebrate Independence Day as the rest of the USA did.

Let us return to the evening of the second day and the twilight attack against Culps Hill. We know that Sergeant Fred Durbin's 78th Regiment was part of Slocum XII Corp defending this flank, and lost ground across Spangler's field; we also know he was killed and first buried in a trench on Spangler's field where the defenders were over-run. It is most likely that he was killed on this evening.

After the battle with the Armies departed, the little town was faced with a terrible task. It was high summer and the battleground was littered with over ten thousand dead, and of course, in addition many dead horses and mules. The US Government made an immediate decision to purchase seventeen acres of land, and with the help of civilian volunteers entrained in from far and wide, temporary trenches were dug and hasty burials took place until the site could be formally laid and dedicated as a permanent national cemetery.

Finally, this was completed and a dedication ceremony arranged for 19th November of that year. It took place as planned, many of the wounded still there attended. A leading politician made an oration as was popular in those days and the President also attended. The orator spoke for over an hour with many classical illusions, then the President said a few words. Today the Orator's fine speech is forgotten, but most Americans can recite at least some of the Abraham Lincoln's Gettysburg address.

The graves are arranged in semi circles with a large memorial at the hub. The largest number of graves belong to the New York State Regiments who formed the biggest contingent in the Union Army.

One grave stands a little way from the others. It is that of Jenny Wade, the only civilian killed, struck by a stray bullet. When she died she had just received a letter from her Fiancé in the Union Army; she did not know he had been killed in the Shenandoah Valley a few days before.

Today the National Memorial Park is beautifully kept, the grass is mown, the scattered trees are inhabited by many colourful blue jays and here and there stands the occasional long silent cannon. So it was a thoughtful occasion for my Wife and I to stand there by the long rows of gravestones many marked with the single word "Unknown", and think of the tragic times that brought a Clevedon lad over three thousand miles to die on a hill far away.

Brian Wood

❑ ❑ ❑ ❑ ❑

A Boyhood on the Beach

Recollections of Clevedon and life in the 20's to 30's

My Grandparents were managers of the Royal Pier Hotel in the late 1800's, and my aunt, Miss Klemm, was well known to all those folks who visited the confectionery counter at the Towers Cafe. My parents and I lived in the Beach Cafe in the 1920's and 30's. They managed the business for Mr Frank House, he also owned the Towers and Oaklands Hotel, and previously, the Creamery on Hill Road. We took over from Mr Seager, who as he left, moved out a flock of hens from our future kitchen garden. Being very young, I was to find many years interest in our new home. It all seemed very changeless and permanent at the time. The house was late Regency in style, comprising a cellar and two stories and attics, with cafe and shop included. Lawned and bordered in front, it had large gardens containing a disused well at the back. The stone-flagged cellar included a kitchen, scullery, coke/coal and other store rooms. The kitchen had a rope operated dumb-waiter lift to the two upper floors. The scullery had a baker's oven and a hand operated water pump over a low sink. Only once, as the result of a heavy storm, did the pump ever work, then water gushed out of it, overflowing between the cellar flag-stones and covering the floor to a couple of inches depth. The house had two topmost rooms with attic windows, one was used by Mrs Walker of Pinehurst in Bellevue Road as an oil painting Artist's Studio. The first floor [above the shop] had the usual bedrooms and a tea room. When we first moved in, the lavatory was typically Victorian and fitted with a seat the full width of the room. No bathroom, and only a hand-basin in an adjoining room for customers. This was typical of Clevedon houses of that time.

The ground floor comprised the shop, a still room with an old-fashioned 'Clevedon 94' pedestal telephone, a pantry and a room with an ice-cream store cabinet made by Frigidaire. The freezer box of this was completely separate from the motor/compressor unit. Before the fridge was installed, ice-cream had to be made down in the 'cool' cellar, using a machine with a handle and double container. The ice-cream mix was put into the inner container and ice [supplied by Mr House the fishmonger at Exeter House in Old Church Road] with freezing salt added, filled the space between the inner and outer containers. A lot of hassle. Milk was delivered twice a day in summer by Maynard's from the Hill Road Creamery, and our post was delivered morning and afternoon, and Christmas Day, by a postman wearing a peaked helmet. The staff we employed always came from the Village area from old Clevedon families. The town was kept busy in summertime by visitors in Bed and Breakfast, Apartments and Board Residence accommodation, mainly arriving by train at the G.W.R. station. Campbell's had a fleet of paddle pleasure steamers with frequent trips from the pier. Most of the visitors were older retired folks, and they often paid return visits. Clevedon didn't have a marine lake until about 1931, so apart from the August fair in Salthouse Field most of the seaside activities were on the beach near the Pier. The annual swimming gala, a diving board and greasy pole being set up on the Pier Rocks; possibly a short water polo match organised, all depending on a short state of high tide. Some of the outboard motor speedboats were hydroplanes.

Plying the usual slipway boat trade would be Joe Rich's 'Y-NOT', Captain Rowles's 'PRIMROSE' [a converted ship's lifeboat] and Mr Gibson's 'AUDREY'. Their trips would take you either beyond Wains Hill, or up channel to Ladye Bay, returning by an out-to-sea route. Free trips held the fascination for us boys in seniority 'pecking order'. Holding the boat to the slipway and collecting petrol from Yarde's or Binding's Beach Garages qualified you [as long as you didn't get them mixed up] for a trip. You then sat in the cockpit with the skipper. The Beach offered charabanc tours with coaches owned by Yarde and Binding and Payne. Ice-cream was sold by the Fortune family and other vendors, from two or three barrows alongside the promenade pavement. Cars were very few and far between, except later at the week ends and summer holiday periods. There used to be a cabstand near the pier before the under-prom shelter was built. At the alcoves site, there was a glass shelter and the Alcoves Concert Party 'Pavilion'. The family concert party performed during the July and August summer season afternoon and evenings. The Bandstand on the Green Beach provided a summer orchestra, and sometimes, the Clevedon Town Silver Band. The first Monday in August [Bank holiday] was Hospital Carnival Procession Day. Led by 'Drum Major' Len Blackmore, the local floats and other entrants were supported by the Town and Salvation Army Bands, and possibly a band from Bristol. They started at East Clevedon and went via the Triangle, West End and the the Beach to finish at Herbert Gardens, with sideshows, drinks, prize giving, confetti fights and a firework display. I was twice awakened by my parents when we lived on the Beach, to be shown the night time glow of fires, seen beyond Oaklands and the Bandstand. The first time was when the Chalet Tearooms [now Salthouse Toilets site] burnt down; the other when the Weston-super-Mare Grand Pier was consumed by fire.

A more pleasant event was the early morning sight, across the channel towards Wales, of the Airship R100 en-route for Canada, shining silver in the sunlight. One day, it must have been about 1930, certainly before the work on the Marine Lake was begun; it was in the morning, and I was in our sitting room looking out to sea, the tide being completely out. A light bi-plane aircraft landed on the big sandbank that extended from the region of the pier head to Salthouse Point, where the old summerhouse stood. The aircraft landed on the sandbank and then took off again. Then later it tried again, but was unable to take off the second time. It had to be rescued from the shore and pulled to the Beach by some men. I never found out; but I presume it was rescue help from Willcocks' West End Garage. The size of the sandbank became reduced over the years, after the lake was built. During the long fine summer evenings [we forget the others] the arrival of the Sunday pleasure boats from Wales were always a source of interest. There must have been hundreds of passengers from Cardiff and Newport who came ashore to visit the various public houses from the Royal Oak to the village pubs, and later, to the Salthouse Hotel. The pubs in Wales being shut on a Sunday, Campbell's Steamers always did a lucrative business from Wales to Somerset. The fun began with the last minute scamper from all of the hostelries, up through the town and along the whole length of the Beach from Salthouse to the Pier. T he Pier Master always sounded the bell at Toll-house ten minutes before the boat sailed; but the crowds would be dashing along the Beach, while the Captain was sounding his ships whistle impatiently on leaving, people continuing to make for the pier as the boat was leaving. As it was Sunday there were few trains back to Wales.

Winter evenings always seemed very long in those days, the streets were very dark and only poorly illuminated by very sparse and dim lighting. Coming home from Choir Practice at Christ Church, or from an evening out at St John's Hall or the Picture House was quite a scaring experience, especially hastening as quickly as possible past Rawlings the undertakers on the last leg home; and then what glory to get into the light and warmth of home. It was particularly eerie on those dark foggy nights, with the mournful moaning of the foghorn from the lightship anchored on the Welsh Grounds in the channel and the occasional answer of the odd ship's siren. A friend who left with you would often drop into his home on the way, leaving you to do the last half mile on your own, it was quite common to see no-one else for the rest of the journey, unbelievable today. The shop used to close early in the winter time; as no-one was about after dusk. Before closing time the lamp lighter would arrive along the Beach with his bicycle and ladder to light the very few Beach Gaslights. Daytimes there might be a visit from the muffin man, with his bell and baize covered tray of muffins and crumpets. There were also occasional visits from the knife grinder and a street barrel organ from time to time, as Clevedon lived in an earlier age. The

Clevedon Sunday routine was Church Choir morning and evening, as in those days Sunday was strictly for church attendance. The roads were deserted on Sunday mornings except for people on their way to church and the numerous bells from the Friary, St Peter's, Christ Church and St Andrew's could be clearly heard on the Beach. The Salvation Army band service was a Sunday morning feature in Copse Road, and on Sunday evenings they played on the Beach opposite Brunswick House. We were only allowed to wear our best clothes on Sundays and on Christmas Day. Near the Alcoves and on the Green Beach old ladies used to hand out tracts, whilst by the Alcoves glass shelter Mr Orchard from Copse Road had his Colporteur stand [a wheeled truck with a glass display stand on top] where he sold bibles and tracts. On the Summer Sunday evenings, all the adults seemed to head for the Green Beach to promenade past the Bandstand. By the Flag-staff in the evening there would be a service with a harmonium accompaniment for the hymn singing. Our running around or playing on the Beach was frowned on, on Sundays. My best time was after evening summer choir, when, with fellow choir members Binding, Ware and Bryant we made off through the fir-woods, to Walton Castle [then completely un-restricted] to run around to our hearts content on a glorious summer evening at about eight o'clock. I can picture it in mind's eye now, with the channel glistening in the evening sunlight. In our own homes piano playing was beginning to die out; although you could still hear ardent though uninspired piano practice going on as you passed the odd music teacher's home. This usually took the form of scales and arpeggios. Older folks still continued to play the harmonium and American organ on Sundays. By 1930 we had bought a wind-up portable gramophone [I have those original records on tape today] By 1933 we had borrowed a battery suitcase portable 'Wireless', then purchased a wood cabinet transportable Mc'Michael by 1934 to hear King George the 5th's Christmas speech. Basic programmes were a daily service and doleful music in the morning, then the station would close down until the afternoon time for Children's Hour. Then the Reuters' News and Fat Stock prices. The brightest Sunday evening programme was the Palm Court Orchestra. On Radio Normandy and Luxemburg you could always get livelier popular music, and sponsored programmes such as "The Ovaltinies." On Boxing day [never on Christmas Day] we amused ourselves with family afternoon concerts, in which relatives from Bristol took part. The adults would dance to the gramophone, or otherwise perform. The girls would dress up in spangled dresses, and perform dances they had learned at dancing class. Yours truly would reluctantly recite short school poems, or sing a carol, and usually finish up dressed in 'Drag' causing the more bawdy Aunts much amusement. Winter was not all dull though. We attended local concerts at the Church-Hall Marson Road, performed by the older children of the National School. They appeared very good at the time, and were directed by Miss Mabel Gould and her sister. One act I can still remember was a 'Skeleton Dance' We used to do both school plays and attend concerts at St John's Hall, being a pupil at St John's School at the time. A 'one-off' pantomime was presented by Mr Cox at the Picture House, usually after Christmas. The

Robinson Crusoe Pantomime there was captivating, until later on when I was taken to the Prince's Theatre in Bristol to see Jean Colin in their production, with the marvellous transformation scenes and rough sea effects. My experience of acting in Clevedon School plays are with mixed feelings of excitement and anti-climax. At St John's I was given a two persons 'Trivia' play, with singing, about a King and Queen disagreeing; followed by a 'mummers' play with several characters. I was Be-el-ze-bub, and I seem to recall other characters in 'Blackface' and an 'Eastern Potentate' with school fellows, Morris, Rowley, Binding etc. Needless to say two plays on the first night proved too much. I jumped a cue-line, leaving the Headmaster, Mr Buxton with his eyes and arms raised in anguish to heaven, standing in the wings. Later on, at the Highdale Secondary Modern School worse, to be told off in front of the whole school for my long opening speech in 'As You Like It', a beast of a speech, with my opening co-actor Binding. My fault; not his. We used to take a lot of 'stick' in those days. and only one scholarship in a class of thirty per year if you were lucky. Being fairly new, the school offered science and woodwork besides academic subjects, and Domestic Science for the girls:- quite a good school. Clevedon in those days was a self-contained town, with its own Urban District Council whose events and meetings were reported in great detail in the Mercury. People were employed in family shops and trades, with domestic staff in the larger houses and nursing homes. Industry was local; the Brickworks, Gas Works, Clevedon and Portishead Laundry, Boot Works, and latterly Holland's Pottery and Hale's Bakery. Our supplies of lemonade for the cafe came in bottles with a 'pinch' at the top and a glass marble inside, supplied by Godfrey Archer's Mineral Water Works of Griffin Road. The resident population at that time included many older or retired people. Some larger houses in Walton-St-Mary and central Clevedon were occupied by ex-colonial, professional and clerical families. The remainder of the population followed employment in shops, factories, farming or other trades. Many of the wives gave accommodation to the holiday visitors of which there were many. Our Local schooling started at 9a.m. to 9.20, finishing at 4p.m. to 4.30 depending on the age grade of the school. The lunch break was from 12 to 2.p.m. giving time to walk the three quarters of a mile each way to get home to dinner and back again, as schools were all in the village and East Clevedon area. Later on when the Highdale Secondary Modern School was opened, pupils used to come by train from Congresbury and Yatton, by cycle from Kenn, and also from Tickenham and the Wraxall side of Nailsea, all without state transport. Summer holidays always seemed idyllic for us boys living on or near the Beach, They were shared with neighbourhood school friends, and those from the village. We spent the time model boat sailing in the paddling pool, and the pool by the old baths. We caught crabs from the slipway, using 'bait' supplied free, by Mr Jones the Alexandra Road fishmonger. At ten years old Mick Barrett and I were allowed to fish from the pier by Mr Gibson the pier master. We caught gluey, bony conger eels, later cooked by our mothers, using two-penny herrings bought from Mr Jones. The pier seemed a much more secure place in 1932. Our alternative was river fishing for minnows, sticklebacks, and sometimes tadpoles, in the Land Yeo behind the Picture House. The river was open to the sky then, and ran crystal clear and unpolluted. You could stand on the narrow pavement to the right of the Cinema, by the rustic bridge to Heaven's bungalow, and see down in the open clear river the fish among the water weed. At other times a few of us would get together to play boys' cricket on the green of the Pier Copse, or climb up into the trees in the Alexandra Gardens. There used to be a visiting accordion band there in the summer, and a local male voice choir in the rustic bandstand halfway up the gardens. We would sometimes be sent 'out of the way' as far as the East Clevedon fields at spring time, to pick wild flowers. There, in the fields between Bennett's Ripple and Holly Lane, would be cowslips and primroses, and bluebells in the private Walton Woods ready for the picking. Up into the Walton Manor Woods, we could be shouted at by the gamekeeper, until we reached the top of the woods on to the fields now Edward Road and Edward Road South; where 'innocent' we made haste for home. Summer picnics were enjoyed in the Woodland which extended from the top of the Zig-Zag to the old summerhouse above the Friary. All fields, with some woodland, from the Zig-Zag to Robin Lane (just beginning) to Old Park House, to the Firwoods, to St Edith's Orphanage. Our other picnic venue was Ladye Bay, where two freshwater springs gushed out of the cliffs, clear and fresh for drinking. About the year 1933 we had Keesey's fun fair in their grounds at the Salthouse Hotel. Always good for a visit, it had a tattoed barker who was either/or a Sword Swallower and Fire Eater. He stood at the top of the concrete steps leading down from the.Esplanade to the fairground. The fair consisted of Dodgem Cars, a Kiddie's Roundabout, a Palmist and numerous game sideshow booths. Some years later there was to be a concert party with a specially constructed stage, on the hillside of the Salthouse woods above. We used to watch at the sides 'for free', much to their disgust until (as Derek Lilly reminded me) they blanked the side off with hessian sacking so you had to pay to see. This fair was not connected to Heale's annual August Salthouse Fields Fair The Clevedon seafront of that era was unspoiled, the Green Beach was set out with small plantations of trees and clumps of 'Victorian' shrubs and hedges surrounded by wooden rustic fences. Clumps of these bushes followed along the side of Elton Road. Rustic fences were along the cliff-tops and there were lots of seats everywhere for visitors and old people. With a more compact size and a population of 7,000 there were many open spaces, copses, gardens, with parkland and sheep around Clevedon Hall grounds up to Victoria Road and the Donkey Path. Dial Hill had open farmland fields to Bella Vista [unknown now] and quite a bit of the Walton Park area was fields. At that time of course Walton St Mary was a separate Parish. The late Edmund Shopland had a saying 'The brooks and streams of one's youth, become the mighty rivers of old age' but nevertheless living in Clevedon in those days, we felt we were truly dwelling in a golden time.

Ray Lumbard

❑ ❑ ❑ ❑ ❑

The Marchant Mystery

In the normal detective story, there is a mystery laid out with various clues, which the reader uses, to try and out guess the author's plot. In the Marchant Mystery we have no answers unfortunately, and must rely on guesswork to help in our efforts to unravel the case.

In 1859 Mr Hazell, a butcher, who owned the property previously occupied by Joseph Tyley, the blacksmith; in the Triangle, put in plans for the building of three shops, on the corner of the Triangle/Old St. They were originally called Provident Place; but over the years, with typical Clevedon word mangling, the buildings became known as Providence Place.

It would appear that he sold those parts of the garden remaining, which stretched down as far as the river Land Yeo, so that other people could also develop there. Some was sold to Stephen Reeves, the grocer, who was in business at Triangle House, [now Halifax Property Services]. He had Numbers 1,2 & 3 Windsor Place erected, and a cottage, behind Windsor Place, where he also built his coopers workshop. This cottage is now demolished, and the other places are 16, 18 and 20 the Triangle. Two plots by the river, now Cornerstone and Clevedon Carpets, were sold to Goodland a butcher who was in business at Copse Vale House in Copse Road.

Mrs Marchant was left to bring up a young family on her own

Shortly after this, we hear for the first time of a Beer House called "The First Bell and Exeter Inn".

B.O.H Minutes 7th Dec. 59.

'Mr Varder attended and complained of a nuisance arising through want of a proper urinal at Marchant's premises. The Committee were ordered to inspect the same & report to the next meeting.

This Pub name is connected with Railway Engines, and is quite understandable, as the Railway Station lay less than 50 yards away. The owner of the beerhouse was Mrs Mary Goodland, of Torrington, in Devon, and the licensee was Mr George Marchant.

George Purnell Marchant, brought his family to Clevedon from Weston-super-Mare. He was a stonemason, and came to work on the many new buildings, and possibly even on that of the new Beerhouse, and River Cottage, which was next door. [Now number 26, or Clevedon Carpets.]

Alice Marchant, their eldest daughter, is down in the 1871 Census, as having been born in Weston.s.Mare in 1856. John Marchant, the eldest son, is stated to have been born in Clevedon in 1858. As John is not in the St. Andrews register, we must assume that he was baptised at Weston; possibly his parents had at that time, no intention of living permanently in Clevedon.

What is certain, is that when their third child, Mary Jane Marchant, was baptised at St. Andrews Church, on March 20th 1859; George had put his trade down as Mason. The Marchant's next child Ellen Augusta, baptised June 10th 1860; shows his occupation had changed from Mason, to Innkeeper.

Other children followed:—

Tom Purnell Marchant	Mar 16th 1862
George Purnell Marchant	May 1st 1864

In 1864 first Ellen Augusta, aged only 4 years old, and then Mary Jane, aged 3, the Marchant's two youngest daughters, were buried at St. Andrews Church on the 12th Jan and 17th Jan respectively. George Marchant, their father; at the age of only 37, was buried 28th April. What epidemic caused the 3 deaths we do not know. One of the most prevalent winter illnesses of that time, was bronchitis, which so often turned into pneumonia, with mostly fatal results.

The poor sanitation of Clevedon, was also responsible for many deaths. The following quote, from the Sanitation Report of 1851, will give some idea of the situation. Witness Mr Thomas Somerton, is speaking of the water supply from the village pump:-

"—— This pump is in connexion with the Land Yeo, it being placed only a few feet from the stream, and there being ***a pipe, laid on from the bed of the stream.*** [My bold type D B Lilly] *In the event of the river being polluted by drainage, the public supply of water would be affected."*

Things were still not a great deal better than this in 1864, as the Local Board of Health were continually having to remonstrate with landlords, about the poor sanitary conditions in which their tenants still lived, 13 years after the original report.

Whatever the cause of the deaths was, it left Mrs Marchant with the problem of managing "The First Bell and Exeter Inn" and also looking after a daughter of 8, a son of 6, another son of 2, and a baby boy of only a few days old, baptised in fact within three days of his fathers funeral.

Things must have gone reasonably well for the family in spite of the tragic loss, as the 1871 Census entry has for the beerhouse, the following:-

Mary Ann Marchant	Head	Widow	42
	Beer house keeper		W.s.M.
Alice Marchant	Daughter	Single	15
			Weston.s.Mare
John Marchant	Son		13
			Clevedon
Thomas Purnell Marchant	Son		9
			Clevedon
George Purnell Marchant	Son		7
			Clevedon
George Parsons	Lodger	Single	30
	Butcher		Clevedon

By this time her husband George, had been dead for 7 years, and she seems to have coped with the business successfully. The next time we have notice of the family is a in report in the Clevedon Mercury of July 31st 1875 "On Wed [28th July] evening an accident of a serious nature occurred to John Merchant, [Marchant] son of Mrs Merchant of the First Bell Inn occasioned by the accidental discharge of a gun which was about to be used for the destruction of sparrows in a field in the proximity of the Co-operative stores - - the charge appears to have entered the poor young fellows mouth and completely blown away one cheek. Mr Pizey was promptly in attendance but as the sufferer was a member of the Patriots Friendly Society handed the case over to the surgeon of the club Dr. Skinner, under whose care he is progressing as favourably as he can with such a serious injury."

The Co-operative stores was at that time at the bottom left side of Queens Rd. In 1875 what was referred to as a 'Rook and Rabbit' rifle by A Henry of Edinburgh (Pictorial History of the Rifle; GWP Swenson, pub. Ian Allan Ltd. 1971) had a bore of .360in. which is larger than the .303 of the army of 39-45. It is most likely therefore that the lad was using light shot-gun. The spread of the shot pattern would mean that the gun would have been in extremely close range for it to have 'entered his mouth'. The words used when they wrote that the charge 'blew away one cheek' shows in my opinion that it was a charge of shot, and one wonders if perhaps the young man was in fact for some reason or other, attempting to commit suicide? Why this should be is the first of the unexplainable mysteries, for a 17 year old to want to do this, suggests that there is some extreme trouble worrying him. However there is no mention in the newspaper report of any other person having been present, and the chance of accidentally discharging a gun so close to his face is very unlikely.

The next time we hear of Mary Ann Marchant is a news item in the Clevedon Mercury 19th May 1877, it simply said :-

"Long Ashton sessions yesterday, before E J Daubeny, R Godwinson, H Elton & H J Mirehouse Esq. Money Lending Case. Mrs Marchant was committed for trial in this case, but admitted to bail in two sureties,of £10 pounds each."

The following week we learn more.

Mercury May 26th 1877

Obtaining money under false pretences.

Last week we were obligated to abbreviate this case which was as follows. Mrs Mary Ann Marchant of the First Bell Inn; Clevedon; was summoned to the Long Ashton Petty Sessions of Friday last by Mr George Powell of 6 Loughlin Terrace Redland; and charged with obtaining from him on the 28th of February last, the sum of £30 under certain false pretences, with intent to cheat and defraud.

The circumstances of the case appeared to be these. The complainant advanced the defendant on the 28th of February last, the sum of £30 under certain conditions. —— the defendant said she paid her rent half yearly, and that she owed nothing until the 25th of March. She produced a receipt of £17...10 shillings, dated on or about the 12th October 1876, for a half years rent due the 29th of September prior, with a stamp affixed thereto, and the name of Mr Alonzo Dawes, the Agent for the landlady written across it.

On the 13th of February last, the defendant executed a bill of sale for £85, which was duly filed on the 28th of the same month; and in consequence thereof, an execution was afterwards levied by Mr Powell, and distress levied by the Agent to the Landlady for £17...10shillings; the half years rent due to the 29th of September last, and an undertaking was given to pay, subject to the claim being a legal one. Mr Carter, instructed by Mr Thick, appeared to prosecute, and the evidence of Mr Powell having been taken, Mr Knapp, clerk to Mr Thick, proved seeing the defendant make and sign a statutory declaration. She told Mr Thick that she had not given any charge on her furniture; —— The Mortgage deed was also executed by the defendant at the same time; the money was then handed to her by a cheque.

Mr Thomas Hazelwood, stated he was a money lender residing at 12 Wilson Street, Bristol; and he knew the defendant, to whom he lent money on a bill of sale dated the 13th of February 1877, which he produced, and which was signed by the defendant in his presence; it was for £85. £77 of which remained unpaid. It was registered on the 28th of February. He lent her a portion of the money to pay her rent, and she sent him a receipt for half a years rent, due the 29th of September last; purported to be signed by the agent Mr Dawes.

Mr Alonzo Dawes, stated that he was an auctioneer living at Clevedon, and he was agent to Mrs Goodland who lives near Liverpool; the owner of the Public House occupied by the defendant. He had frequently applied to her for rent previously to Xmas last, but had never received any. The receipt produced was not in his writing or his signature.

Witness had received half a years rent from Mr Clark, an auctioneer, who sold the defendants goods under an execution. The defendant having been cautioned, reserved her defence, and was committed for trial at the next quarter sessions, but admitted to bail.

Case No 32 at Quarter sessions July 1877 [Bundle Q/S 708] and tried before T E Rogers and T Thring Esqs.

Mary Ann Marchant
[Exeter Inn, Clevedon Triangle]
ON BAIL. trade none.

Came before E J Daubeny Esq., Cornwallis Crescent, Clifton, Bristol; and another, at Long Ashton, and remanded for quarter sessions. Date of Warrant 18th May. Charged with:-

Obtaining by false pretences from George Powell, the sum of thirty pounds his monies, with intent to defraud him of the same, at Clevedon, on the 28th February 1877.

Evidence was read from the witnesses statements. The defendant said when asked "I have nothing to say." She was accordingly found guilty, of obtaining money by false pretences. As she had no previous convictions, she was sentenced to six weeks hard labour at Shepton Mallet.

Whilst in Shepton Mallet she would have been on Class Three Diet:-Convicted Prisoners employed at Hard Labour for terms exceeding twenty one days, but not more than six weeks; — and convicted prisoners not employed at Hard Labour for terms exceeding twenty one days and not more than four months.

Males	Females
Breakfast	
1pt Oatmeal Gruel, 6 oz. Bread	
Dinner	
Sunday, Tuesday, Thursday and Saturday	
3 oz. cooked Meat without Bone	
8 oz. Potatoes,	8 oz. Potatoes
8 oz. Bread	6 oz. Bread
Dinner	
Monday Wednesday Friday	
1pt Soup,	1pt Soup
8 oz. Bread	6 oz. Bread
Supper As Breakfast	

There was no 'Green' food provided even for longer term prisoners. When we consider that even in the Royal Navy of fifty years earlier, there was a recognition that no green food or fruit, quickly led to scurvy and that to counteract this the Navy issued the sailors lime juice; one wonders why the prisoners were not given some form of food containing vitamin 'C'.

In the sums involved £85, and £30, we have in today's equivalent, something like £23,000, this does not reckon in the value of the unpaid rent for the lease. What happened to the money, and why it was needed, never became clear. Was it in any way connected to the trouble which her son John had had, in 1875?

There was a reference in the statement of one of the witnesses, George Powell, that she had told him she still had two and a half years to run, of a lease of 21 years. This would put the lease as being from 1859; which confirms our conclusion as to when the place was built. The witness continued "I asked her who had the lease? She said a relative who lived at Weston." Had she mortgaged the lease, and had to have money to pay it back? The Mysteries are still unsolved.

In the Long Ashton Petty Sessions licensed premises record book P/S/cl 1/3 there is a note.

1877 September The First Bell and Exeter Inn; Mary Goodland, Torrington, Devon; owner; Mary Ann Marchant, tenant; Mary Ann Marchant, was indicted at the Somerset Quarter Sessions on the 3rd of July, for obtaining money under false pretences, and sent to gaol for 6 weeks; and the licence, was not asked to be renewed.

The 1881 Census has a return for Lime Kiln Lane :-

Marchant Mary Ann
SJ178 I Lime K. L. Head W 52
Laundress Clevedon

Marchant John SJ178 Son S 23 Mason Clevedon

Marchant Tom SJ178 Son S 19 Mason Clevedon

Marchant George SJ178 Son S 17 General Labourer Clevedon

Then we hear about Mary Ann for the last time, from the Burials Register, at St. Andrew's Church.

Marchant, Mary Ann. 69 35 Brighton Rd., Redland, Bristol. 17th Apr. 1900

Her daughter remained single, and is accounted for in due course.

Marchant, Alice Melinda. 79 Redland, Bristol. 28th Oct. 1935

It would seem that the family had moved to Bristol. "The First Bell and Exeter Inn" became Somerset House. The shop of the well known Clevedon business man Frederick Parker, Baker & Confectioner. He moved there from Watledge House, number 7 Old Church Road. Later he had the present WH Smith's premises built, It was for a time the Conservative Club until the new premises were built over the road on the site of Brookdale House. Later he had Danesbury House built, at No 4 Ken Road, and moved his business there, utilising part of the old mews of Brookdale House as his bakery.

Derek Lilly

❑ ❑ ❑ ❑ ❑

Wareham's Guide of 1878

We thought that our readers might find interesting this extract from Wareham's Clevedon Guide of the 1878, giving as it does a picture of Clevedon which no-one alive today will recognize. I have put my additions clarifying places etc., in square brackets.

At the commencement of the present century [1800] the whole of Clevedon was comprised in the Court (with its dependencies), the Vicarage (which was then adjacent to the Parish Church), a few farm houses, and the cottages of the peasantry. Of middle class private dwellings there were none, and, so far as we can learn, Clevedon at that date possessed neither a "lawyer" nor a "doctor". Elysian condition of society to have lived [in?] without the advocacy and assistance of either.

It is rather difficult, gentle reader is it not? to imagine Clevedon when there were no roads, no houses, no gas lamps, when there was no railroad and no coach, when there was no newspaper; and when the genius of solitude reigned, and when the venerable Parish Church, complacently looking out from its sequestered nook, might have appropriated to itself the well-known stanza of Cowper:-

'I am monarch of all I survey,
My right there is none to dispute;
From the centre all round to the Sea.'

Yet such was Clevedon in the so-called 'Good old times'.

1800-10

It will much facilitate our purpose if we now divide the time into decades. i.e. periods of ten years each, as it will enable us the better to trace with accuracy the gradual development of the town. And we may observe that for the dates from January, 1863, we are chiefly indebted to the valuable 'Calendar of Events' in the Clevedon Almanac, published by Mr Gear Jas Caple at the Mercury & Courier Office, Clevedon. During this very primitive period Old Clevedon, with its population of 334 souls, lay in snug repose at the foot of the surrounding eminences, undisturbed by the ring of the mason's trowel or the sound of the carpenter's saw, for the spirit of ambition had not then tempted it to climb the adjacent hills and court the admiration of beholders for its modern structures. Very unsophisticated were its inhabitants, and very primitive were their habits, tastes, and occupations. There were no sowing and reaping machines in those days, and steam ploughing was undreamed of. Then might have been realised the poetic description of Gray:-

"The curfew tolls the knell of parting day,
The lowing herd winds slowly o'er the lea;
The ploughman homeward plods his weary way,
And leaves the world to darkness and to me.
Now fades the glimm'ring landscape on the sight,
And all the air a solemn stillness holds,
Save where the beetle wheels his drony flight,
And drowsy tinklings lull the distant folds."

Then no gas illumined the darkness of night, and no hurrying cabs and rumbling omnibuses tearing away from the screaming trains with their freights of weary homeward bound travellers disturbed the tranquillity of the ruminating native. And Clevedon consisted only of the Court, the Vicarage, the farmhouses, and the labouring rustics.

1810 - 1830
(Being a period of two decades)

Inland dwellers are ever delighted with a visit to the seaside, and a bathe in its health giving waters. To this, Clevedon is no doubt indebted for the first impulse it received. The overcrowded inhabitants of the neighbouring city of Bristol were quickly alive to its attractions, and the demand for accommodation soon met with a ready supply.

About 1822 the Rock House was built by Mr [Thomas] Hollyman, the proprietor of the Old Inn. The *Union Independent Chapel* was erected in 1827 at the bottom of the steep slope leading from Christ Church to the Old Village, now called Chapel Hill. About this time the *Bristol Inn* was built. On or about the year 1828 was built the original *Royal Hotel*, where, as the chronicler relates, *'Comfortable accommodation is combined with reasonable charges.'* *Prospect House*, near Christ Church, appears to have been the first dwelling house built on the hill. Then was erected a villa residence now known as Newton House [not so, this was built much later] which was soon followed by the erection of Nightingale Villa, Champion House and the Marine Villas on the slope of the hill towards the sea.

So rapid had been the growth that by 1828 no less than forty new houses had been built, and as many more were in the course of building. Some of these now constitute the row of dwellings on the beach, and others ·Wellington Terrace, which commands a very pleasing view of the coast; in the foreground are 'Fertile fields interspersed with copses extending to the sea, with the Church picturesquely situated on the romantic promontory forming the southern side of the bay' These fertile fields are now covered with handsome dwellings. By this time Hill Road had been made, beautifully undulating along the limestone ridge and leading to several pleasantly situated lodging houses of recent erection. Hot Baths had also been built by 'an industrious Speculator'. In this decade was built the York Hotel, intended as a boarding house for the upper class of visitors. It is now known as Leagrove. A few dwellings were erected in the Copse Road, one of which was occupied by 'Rose's Library'.

1830 - 1840

In 1831 the population had increased to 1,147. Clevedon was now becoming more extensively known and social life developed in an increasing ratio. A stage coach plied between Bristol & Clevedon daily in the summer, and once or twice a week in the winter. A receiving house for letters was opened at the shop of the late Mr Edmund Gurney. [Melrose House] More bathing machines were called into requisition on the beach. Pill Pilots would put in to Clevedon, and, after refreshing themselves at the primitive 'Rock House', take visitors for a sail on the channel, or a days excursion to the Holmes. Theirs were strong seaworthy boats, having no such luxury as a cabin, but open to the weather, fitted with three portable masts and sails, and being as the owners said:- 'Like ducks upon the water'. Their owners were a hardy weather worn race. Saddle donkeys caparisoned with white cloths, also afforded inspirating fun for the children, and often no little merriment for the adults, as they watched the 'Donkey Women' or 'Donkey Boys' belabouring the 'Patient' donkeys that would not go, but which would occasionally take to lying down and rolling off their juvenile riders to the ground; and sometimes a saddle's girth would give way and land some hapless demoiselle upon her feet in a bewilderment of consternation. There were no donkey chairs in those days. The cornerstone of Christ Church was laid by Lady Elton on May 29th 1838.

1840 - 1850

In 'Fullarton's Gazetteer' 1840-41 we read, 'A branch railway from Clevedon to Yatton, on the Bristol and Exeter Railway, is contemplated; acres 2,970; population in 1831, 1,147. Poor-rates in 1838 £224 12s 0d.' in 1846 a branch line opened.

1850 - 1860

About this period the Bellvue Boarding Establishment was opened. [1853] It is now occupied by the West of England and South Wales District Bank. [Lloyd's] During the decade extending over 1850 to 1860 the genius of improvement became active.

Salt House became improved into its present attractive condition. A new carriage road was made by the late Sir Charles Elton, Bart., [The top half of Marine Parade] by which the Beach became accessible from the Hill Road by a more gradual descent than Marine Hill or the Copse Road. Several new walks were made, to wit, one through a fir plantation to Strawberry or the Bella Vista Hill, the Bonnie View and Mountain Pass, also a new drive from the North end of Wellington Terrace to Highdale Road. Paths had been previously formed beneath Wellington Terrace and the top of the cliffs to Ladye Bay by the late Sir Abraham and Lady Elton.

Clevedon is indebted to the Elton family for many other most valuable improvements, which have materially aided in gradually developing the natural beauties of the neighbourhood, and rendering them accessible to the residents and visitors.

In 1859 the Clevedon (1st Somerset) Volunteer Artillery Corps was formed. In 1851 the Copse Road Chapel was built. The Local Board was established in April 1853. During this year *Frankfurt Hall* [Clevedon Hall] was built. The new *Congregational Chapel* in Hill Road was built in 1855. The Elton Road was opened in 1855, and Linden Road about 1857.

1860 - 1870

During the decade the following topics may be noted as indicating the steady progress of the town, and increasing value of property. All Saint's Church was consecrated in 1860. In April 1863, the rate payers, in meeting assembled, resolved on having a new survey of the Parish. June 2nd a memorial window was placed in the Parish Church in memory of the late Conrad Finzel Esq. [the builder of Frankfurt Hall] In 1864, Woodfield House and Cottage was purchased at auction for £1,720. October the 5th, the shaft for the Waterworks was sunk near the National School under Sir A H Elton's directions.

1865

Jan 28th. Waterworks Company formed. March 25th the contract for carrying out the sewerage scheme was signed. August 15th Waterworks Reservoir under Dial Hill commenced. 22nd, completion of sewer outlet at the Pill. November 1st, Sir A H Elton proposed the formation of a new walk connecting the Beach with the Green Beach; a great improvement to the locality. 18th, Sir A H Elton proposed to convey to Trustees the piece of land now known as Herbert Gardens. This was a happy thought as it preserves *in perpetuo* a fine open space in the heart of the town, which not only conduces to its ornamentation, but likewise to its health-fullness by preventing that bane of modern towns, overcrowding.

1866

February 22nd, Marlborough House [Now part of Mount Pleasant on the corner of Albert and Victoria roads bought in at auction, at Guildhall Auction Rooms Bristol, for £1,000. 26th, meeting of the Waterworks shareholders; estimated cost of works, £3,622; capital £5,000 in shares at £10 each. May 5th, new sewerage completed; cost £5,346:9s:11d; June 1st, Brecon House bought in at Auction for £1,010. 28th, Sir Arthur Elton presented a clock for All Saint's Church. 24th, proposal for a pier first entertained by influential inhabitants. July 26th, Arundel House bought in at Commercial Rooms, Bristol, for £1,200. Nov.14th, first meeting at Public Hall to discuss the proposed scheme for erecting a pier, when a committee was formed.

1867

Feb 14th, 1867 at a meeting of the pier committee a Board of Directors was formed, and £3,500 subscribed in the room - a practical illustration of public spirit. Mar 23rd. Clevedon Pier prospectus issued; capital £20,000 in £10 shares. May 1st, it was decided to erect a public weighbridge. 4th, the new Pier Share List had reached £7,000. 27th, specifications signed for the construction of the Pier. June 24th, Herbert Subscription Gardens opened. Sept 20th, Vestry Meeting at Parish Church to consider requisition, signed by above fifty influential rate payers, desiring the establishment of a Market. Oct 5th, erection of Friends' Meeting House. 30th, Hillwood House realised £1,005; it is noteworthy that only a few years previously the same property was sold for £750. Nov 2nd, erection of a fountain in the Triangle. Dec 9th, large meeting of rate payers at Public Hall to request the Local Board of Health to exercise their powers to construct a Market House, and bring the town of Clevedon under the operation of the Market Act. Sir A H Elton presented the Parish with a site.

1868

Jan 8th the existing design of the Market proposed by Mr Braikenridge, seconded by Mr Ransford, and decided on at Board of Health Meeting. 24th, the first 100 foot of Pier put into position. Feb 8th, The Village Hall completed. 25th, Village Hall opened, It Cost £264 13s. March 4th, Tenders for erecting the Market for £1,120 and the weighbridge for £269, accepted by the Local Board. 18th, voluntary meeting by the rate payers to protest against the liability of Clevedon to pay poor rates for the Parish of Bedminster. April 25th, demolition of the old Rock House. May 6th, the subject of Slaughter houses first mooted at Local Board meeting. Aug 5th,

600 feet of the new Pier completed. Sept. 5th, Public Baths first suggested by Mr Button. Oct 19th, plans for new Rock Hotel approved at Local Board meeting. Dec 3rd, gas first lit on the Pier. 12th, Messrs. Hamilton & Co completed the erection of the Pier. In this year Salt House was completed in its present state.

1869

Feb 16th, meeting to inspect plans for Public Baths; estimated costs £4,000. Mar 29th, Public Opening of Clevedon Pier; general holiday. Apr 19th, restoration of Walton Old Church [St. Mary's] commenced. June 2nd, committee appointed at Local Board meeting to draw up Pleasure Boat Bye-laws. Sept 22nd, revival of Flower Show, after lapse of years, great success.

1870 -1880

1870

March 16th, Venetian House and Cottage sold at Bristol Hotel for £825. May 7th, permanent enlargement of the Clevedon Mercury and Courier to 48 columns. Nov 3rd, consecration of St. Mary's Church. Aug 3rd, 1871, the Revd Charles Marson, MA. Prebend of Lichfield, inducted to Parish Church, succeeding Rev W N Pedder, who was Vicar of Clevedon for 40 years.

1872

Jan 11th, Oxford House [now Woodbury Elton Road] disposed of for £1,700. Feb 14th, no less than 16,000 Valentines passed through the Local Post Office - a sure indication of an increased population. Mar 8th, a new pumping station at the Water Works completed. 22nd, a deputation waited on the Lord of the Manor (Sir A H Elton, Bart.) and presented him with a petition, 27 feet in length, soliciting the formation of a Local Session. June 20th, Sunhill disposed of for £5,200.

1873

June 14th, Convalescent Hospital established at East Clevedon. 27th, East Clevedon Schools opened. July 16th, Bristol Hotel sold for £1,110. Dec 3rd, new sewerage report read at Local Board meeting; estimated cost £1,731. During the year, 48,000 people went on the Pier - another practical proof of the public regard that Clevedon was obtaining.

1874

Feb 21st, a meeting held to consider the desirability of forming a club in Clevedon. Mar 16th, meeting of Pew Holders, at which it was decided to place an organ in Christ Church. May 26th, Cottage Hospital opened this day. The same day Colonel Cox, Government Inspector, visited Clevedon in reference to the the proposed improvements. June 13th, the New Church for South Clevedon first suggested. Nov 11th, new sewerage works contracted for; cost £1,425. Dec 5th, survey of Midland railway to Clevedon , branch from Portishead and on to Weston-super-Mare for Burnham. 21st, Dedication of Memorial Bell presented to all Saints' Church 'In loving memory of the founder' Dame Rhoda Susan Elton.

1875

Jan. 6th, the subject of taking over the Copses mentioned at the Local Board meeting. Feb 5th, opening of Christ Church Organ; cost £345. Mar 3rd, Sir A H Elton's proposition to hand over the Copses to the Local Board of Health laid on the Board table. 13th, completion of the Promenade improvement contract. 31st, Annual meeting of the Clevedon Cricket Club. May 14th, J. T. Harrison Esq.; made enquiry as to the expenditure of £550 in the purchase of land as pleasure ground. Sir A. H. Elton ultimately generously presented the amount to the Parish for laying out the same. Aug 28th, the progress of the town at this date may be inferred from the amount of business transacted by the Local Board of Health, as represented by the accounts for the year ending March 25th, the total receipts having been £6,599:17s:0½d. whilst the amount of loans remaining unpaid was £9,355:6s:8d. Sept 18th, Contributions in aid of the Clevedon Cottage Hospital to this date, £118:18s:6d. Nov 6th, the new Marine Baths commenced by Mr Vickery.

1876

Jan.25th, Beach House sold for £1,115. Feb 27th, opening of the new organ presented by Conrad Finzel Esq., to the Parish Church. Mar 11th, ground purchased in Linden Road for Skating Rink. Apr 13th, Chandos House and Rodney House sold for £800. Esplanade House for £850, and Grove Villa for £1,060. May 8th, meeting held to consider the enlargement of the Village Hall. May 18th, Royal Hotel bought in for £4,000. June 30th, opening of new skating rink. July 3rd, Sir A. H. Elton gave the piece of land now forming the connecting walk between the Green Beach and Salthouse Beach - a real boon to both residents and visitors. July 30th, opening of the temporary church, locally designated 'The Barn' (now the Library) in South Clevedon. Aug 4th, Royal Hotel re-opened for business. 29th, Clevedon Regatta, after a lapse of 5 years. Sept16th, Pictorial World Clevedon number appeared. Oct 19th, foundation stone of St. John's Church laid.

1877

Feb 6th, Park House sold for £2,000. Apr 4th, plans for new wing to Royal Hotel passed the Local Board. May 1st, the growing wants of the town requiring a larger public hall, meeting held to consider the subject. May 16th Bellvue House, purchased by the West of England and South Wales District Bank. July 14th, prospectus of Clevedon Baths and Lodging House Company issued; capital £5,000 in £5 shares. August 7th, Frankfurt Hall sold for £30,000; estimated cost about £100,000; Frankfurt Lodge realised £1,000. and Salt House was bought in for £3,000. Sept. 13th, plans for the enlargement of the Village hall passed by the Local Board; estimated cost £130. 19th, Archery meeting.

1878

Feb 20th, New Sunday School rooms and Class Rooms to hold 300 people, opened at Copse Road Chapel; cost £800. Mar 8th the Clevedon Marine Baths, having been completed and handsomely furnished, are now thrown open to visitors. April 30th, Church of St. John consecrated.

Derek Lilly

❑ ❑ ❑ ❑ ❑

Clevedon and the Floods

At Clevedon we have the second highest rise and fall of tide in the world. If there was any serious breach of the sea defences at highest tide, the Triangle area would be 4'6" deep in flood water, and the South of the town would be completely covered in the same way.

Before the re-cutting of the Blind Yeo in 1954 it was normal to see the moorland flooded for most of the winter, and even in a wet summer many of the fields were unusable. After a winter as wet as the one 1994-5, it would be quite expected that the road across Nailsea Wall and the lower road over Claverham Drove would be flooded and impassible with only the hedges showing above water level, and any luckless traveller could wind up in the side rhines. A woman who lived in the 'Kenn Pier' area told the writer some years ago, that as a girl she was rowed in a boat across the fields to Tickenham to attend church there one Sunday.

It is understandable then, that the consequences of broken seawalls and the purely temporary inconvenience until they were mended, was more or less taken for granted in the early days of our 'village', and those farms and hamlets which lay to the South of us on the North Somerset moorland.

An illustration from the cover of Edward White's book of 1607

The first recorded disaster we hear of, is in January of 1607, when in the words of a tract published by Edward White of London:-

'Who would not have thought this had bin a second Deluge! for at one time these inhabited places; were sunke clean out of sight. - - - Kenhouse another village covered all over. Kingson a third village likewise lies buried in salt Water. So besides other small cottages standing in Vallies is Brian Downe a village quite consumed. Adde unto these peopled places, the losse of Marshes, Corn-fieldes, Pastures, Meddowes, and so forth, more than can bee numbred: the misery of it no man can Expresse.'

Marked at the back:-*'To be sold att ye signe of the Gunne at the North doore of Pauls Church'* [St. Pauls Cathedral London]

The worst of this flood of 1607 seems to have been concentrated in the Bridgwater Bay area however, and we did not suffer to excess, although there is a record in the porch of Kingston Church which states the facts of the matter, and the depth of the water.

Only 60 years later there is record of another inundation. This was mentioned in the meeting of the Somerset Archaeological Society Proceedings of 1881.

Page 31- Mr Green:- excerpts from his dissertation on the 1667 flood.

There was in Clevedon a farm known as Perry's Marsh Farm [Now called Dowlais Farm] worth about £80 a year. And there belonged to it, a large piece of ground called The Warth adjoining the seashore on the river Severn, but about seven feet higher than the shore, forming a natural bank of earth against the sea, and which had never been repaired by anybody.

Within this marsh ground was a ditch and a bank about three feet high, forming a second barrier. The sea in 1667 destroyed the outer bank and carried away about 4 score acres, several feet in depth, and not only were the other 40 acres left threatened with destruction, but the Marsh Land was also in danger.

The question was who should repair? As the owners of the shore-land refused to do so an action was brought in the exchequer by the inland owners, who alleged that it was the carelessness on the part of the shore owners from not keeping out the 'Woose' soil brought down by the river, that the wall then lay 'lacerated and worn down'

The owners asserted to the contrary and claimed that the whole district should be assessed, as the whole level would be preserved and benefited. The Court declared that this was right and the plaintiffs, not liking the judgement, refused obedience, and as local magnates endeavoured to intimidate their opponents by inflicting a heavy fine for their asserted neglect. Consequently, Mr William Strode and other owners found themselves committed to "Ye Prison of Ye Fleete"

All that is left of this warth today is at the very most ten acres, so in the last hundred plus years we have lost another 30 acres of saltings.

The last really serious flood was at the turn of the century in 1899 and we are indebted to the Clevedon Mercury for a complete account of this.

Extract from the Clevedon Mercury Feb 18th 1899.

The floods of the past week on low-lying parts of Clevedon and the surrounding district have been more extensive than for a number of years past, and have done an immense amount of damage, the full extent of which is scarcely yet realized. They were also marked by a peculiarly sad accident, which occurred during the height of the invading water on Sunday morning, by which the wife of Mr H. J. Sweet, of Dowlais Farm, lost her life, and a man with her had a very narrow escape.

Perhaps the neighbourhood of Kingston Seymour suffered the most, although land in other parishes has been and is submerged, causing in several instances the death of livestock, principally young lambs and calves. The excessive rainfall and storms of the past month or more appear to have thoroughly saturated the land, so much so the what are locally termed 'Rivers' and 'Rhines' have been filled to the top of the banks, and this water, when the high spring tides have been in, has been sent in large volumes over the surrounding country.

But it was the sea itself which caused the most serious flooding and inconvenience, and at the same time afforded grand sights along the seafront of the town when viewed solely as a spectacle. The weather itself has been remarkable, rain, snow, hail, and sleet falling at separate times and together, varied with glimpses of spring like times and severe thunder-storms, of which that on Monday afternoon will be long remembered. Fortunately during the height of the waves the wind has always dropped to nearly a dead calm, and so saved Clevedon's sea front from what would have been almost certain denudation.

Previous to last week many parts of the surrounding country were under water, and it was apparent from the large surfaces of liquid element to be seen from Chapel Hill that dwellers in the moor districts were having a wet time of it. In an outlying part of Clevedon Parish, and along by Kingston Seymour, the sea is kept at bay in ordinary times by what is termed a 'seawall' which consists of a raised bank of soil, stones, stakes, etc., averaging perhaps four to five feet high. In some parts a second 'wall' a field or so distant runs along by the roadside, but those proved inadequate to keep out the tremendous rush of Sunday mornings tide, when the waves rose several feet about the high water mark, and the tide continued to run for some time after it should have turned. Huge waves breasted this wall and broke over it, and it was not long before what had been green fields were converted into raging torrents of salt water, which was constantly being added to, until at one time between three and four feet of water poured over the roadways into the fields, swelling the already overburdened ditches, and carrying devastation wherever it went. Gates leading into pasture land were submerged to the top bar, large baulks of timber were swept away, and the water invaded low-lying dwelling houses, so much so that articles of furniture were washed about, and it became a matter of anxiety and difficulty to save stock from a watery grave.

Persons intent on charitable actions had to wade through the water almost up to their armpits, and even then they were nearly washed off their feet, though they were supposed to be on the roadway, and it was only through knowledge of the country they were enabled to do anything.

Seawall Farm was a lake, and the water flooded other farms in Kingston almost as badly. Wells have become filled with the saltwater, giving rise to much inconvenience. The seawall appears to have withstood the tremendous strain to which it was subjected, but so much water was sent over that it was decided not to run the first tram to Weston-super-Mare on Sunday morning, the rails being covered.

Even when the tide had ebbed to a considerable extent the water still flowed in, and fears began to be entertained of what would happen with the evening's tide, but though this was abnormally high, the waves were quiet in their action. By Monday afternoon the water was clear of the road for some distance, but part of it, just over the Clevedon boundary into the Kingston Parish, was found still impassible, the water being several feet high over it, though draining off, but the water remaining on the land has since broken down a portion of the wall, causing a more rapid subsistence. [Sic]

The sides of the rhines have also in some places given way, carrying stakes into the water, and trees which grew close alongside, which has the effect of still further penning the water. One enterprising towns-man crawled onto the top of a gate on Monday morning - the two top bars only being above water - and had his photo taken 'waiting for the turn of the tide,' but alas for posterity the negative proved to be a faulty one.

On Saturday night a married woman named Avery, wife of a tramway employee living in Kingston Seymour, left a home she had been calling at to walk to her own home. She was advised to take a light, but she did not consider this necessary. She had not proceeded far, however, before she walked into a rhine, and was only rescued just in time to save her from being drowned. She is under medical attention. Other cases are recorded of persons either falling or jumping into the rhines when trying to clear them, but the individuals were of the male persuasion, and able to get out again after receiving complete duckings.

The tides at Clevedon on Sunday and Monday were viewed with interest by large numbers of people. In the morning the waves covered Salthouse Bay, and sent their tops over the asphalt walk and meadow adjoining. Thousands of stones were left on the path as the waves retreated, but though very high the water was not particularly rough. There was also a thunderstorm, with some bright flashes of lightning. In the evening the tide was again above the expected level, but otherwise presented no unusual feature. There was a very severe thunderstorm, though of short duration, about 4.30 on Monday afternoon, accompanied by a tremendous fall of hailstones, which whitened the ground for a brief space. The lightning was again very vivid, and one of the claps of thunder was the heaviest experienced for a long time past, it being immediately overhead, and seeming to shake houses &c., underneath.

A Rough wind from the W.S.W. also sprang up, and numbers of people went on the sea front to watch for high water about 9.30. The wind dropped again, so the spray effects were not so fine as sometimes seen. However, every now and again large masses of water were sent from the wall into the air, and in one or two cases people venturing too near were knocked down by it. The only damage appears to be the removal of a few more coping stones from the edge of the wall. The 'wash' of the water along the shore was particularly noticeable, and the grind of the stones forming the beach formed a suitable accompaniment to the roar of the breakers.

During the height of Sunday mornings floods a very sad accident happened, when Mrs Sweet, wife of Mr H. J. Sweet, of Dowlais Farm, was drowned, the affair casting quite a gloom over the parish of Kingston Seymour, in which parish Mrs Sweet was particularly well known and respected. Mrs Sweet seeing how the water was rising, became anxious as to how a relative of hers would fare, sent a lad to see if the water was high. He reported that it was, and Mrs Sweet then had a pony harnessed to a trap in which, driven by a bailiff named Millet, she set off to pay her a visit.

They had not proceeded far when they came to where about three feet of sea water was rushing over the road. This evidently startled the pony, which swerved, and in an instant the trap and occupants were in the rhine at the side of the road, at a spot where there was seven or eight feet of water. It was just at the termination of the wall shown in our photograph, and the ends of the shafts of the trap can be seen just sticking out of the water as it appeared the following morning.

The deceased apparently sank at once, and was not seen for a few minutes when her body was washed onto an adjoining field, over which water was also flowing at the time. A lad near procured assistance, and William Wall, a labourer, who lives close to the Isolation hospital, hurried to the spot as fast as he could. He there saw Millet struggling, and after procuring a ladder standing at a hay mow near, he was able, with the help of the boy, and at considerable risk to himself, to rescue Millet who was then unconscious. When he was able to turn his attention to Mrs Sweet she was found to be dead.

Mr Reeves had been told of the accident, and he went to Dowlais Farm as quickly as possible, and was able, through a knowledge of first aid he is acquiring, to be successful in his efforts to resuscitate Millet who is progressing favourably. Mr Reeves who is to be commended for the prompt action he took also tried to restore Mrs Sweet, but it was too late. The pony was got out alive. Dr.'s Martin and Hill were in attendance, but could do nothing for the unfortunate woman.

On Tuesday afternoon Dr. S Craddock, the North Somerset Coroner, held his enquiry at Dowlais Farm, into the circumstances of the accident. The Jury were: Messrs. H. Reeves(Foreman) W. G. Sercombe, P. L. Codner, J. F. Latham, R. Ewings, G. Gould, A. Dyer, T. S. Rails, W. H. Wither, G. Rich, A. Type, and W. H. Drewett Sr.

The first witness was Henry James Sweet, who said he was a farmer, and lived at Dowlais Farm. The deceased, Agnes Sweet, aged 45, was his wife. The accident happened at 9.30 on Sunday morning; that was the time the foreman's watch had stopped. Witness was on the farm at the time tending cattle, but in another direction, and he heard of the accident just as they were bringing the body in, which would be about 10a.m. He did not know his wife was going out. The water had come up over the roads and the floods were out very much. He went to the spot himself, and saw the pony cart in the water. The pony was naturally quiet and not given to shying. He believed the water was about three feet deep across the road at the time of the accident, which the pony would have had to go through. It was a very low part, where water came if there were floods, but they rarely got it like it was on Sunday.

By the foreman;

'They never got the water in like that except when the sea came over the sea wall, which was only about three times in his recollection.'

The Coroner;

'What height is the wall?'

The foreman;

'It averaged from three to seven feet. The bank had not given way.'

Witness continuing, said that when he got there his wife had floated out of the ditch on to the land, the wind and current being that way. He should think the ditch was about seven feet deep.

Robert Evans, a boy employed by Mr Sweet, said that on the Sunday morning last, about 9.30 he saw his mistress leave the house in a pony trap driven by Edwin Millet, bailiff on the farm. He stood on some railings and saw the pony trotting on until it came to the beginning of the water. He had been previously sent by his mistress to see the water, and told her it was very deep. He saw the pony when it got to where the water was across the road turn round, and then he saw his mistress get up in the cart as if she was going to jump out.

Then it all vanished and he could see nothing of the trap or occupants. He jumped from the railings and ran in that direction, and when he got to the spot he could just see Millet's head, and the head of the pony above the water, but he could not see his mistress. He looked round for assistance, saw Mr Wall and called to him. He came running up as fast as he could, and sent witness for ropes. Witness helped to get Millet out, and then ran and fetched another halter, and when he came back with that he saw his mistress for the first time. She was in the water, but on the edge of the field opposite. He could only see her cloak and hands.

The water was over his head in some places. He tried to get to his mistress, but failed, and fell into the water, when he grasped a ladder held by Wall, who then sent him, on horseback to inform the police and a doctor. The first time he came back with one rope he saw Mr Wall with a ladder, which he put into the water, and Millet must have caught hold of it. When he was got out Millet was black in the face.

William Wall a labourer, employed by the Urban District Council of Clevedon, said that he lived at the isolation hospital. On Sunday morning the last witness attracted his attention, and he found an accident had happened. The first he saw was Millet in the ditch, and then he saw Mrs

Sweet washed up in the field. It took him perhaps three or four minutes to get to the spot. He saw the pony and trap in the water, the animal's head being just above the surface.

He ran to a hay mow for a ladder with which to get Millet out, and had to get through the water the best way he could. He only saw part of Mrs Sweet's dress, but noticed she was dead as soon as he saw her. He did all he could by himself and got Millet out. He should think deceased was got out of the water within twenty minutes after he was called.

The Coroner said that that was all the evidence. It was one of those cases which was absolutely unavoidable, and it was very sad that the deceased should have risked going through the water when it was so deep. The only guide to the road was some white rails, and he supposed they were almost covered with water, and it was a regrettable thing that the deceased should have ventured through the water knowing it was deep, with an open rhine on one side.

The boy had given them a very clear account, and had told them he saw the pony swerve, and that they all disappeared. The last witness saw her lying by the water overflowing the road, and it was twenty minutes before she was got out. There was no doubt she died from drowning. He had heard that she was going out to visit her sister in law, about whom she felt some anxiety. He could only recommend the jury to return a verdict of that the deceased was accidentally drowned.

The jury returned a verdict accordingly, and added a rider expressing their deep sympathy with Mr Sweet in his bereavement. They afterwards viewed the spot where the accident happened and several of them expressed an opinion that some protective railings were on the wrong side of the road.

Enormous Tidal Wave in the Bristol Channel

An enormous tidal wave swept the Bristol Channel on Sunday Morning, causing rivers to overflow their banks, and submerging vast tracts of low lying country. The Tide at Cardiff was over forty feet, being the highest of the year, and, a stiff westerly wind blowing, an immense volume of water - like a huge wall, as eye-witnesses describe it - rolled up the river and embankments, and spread like a raging sea over the land. At Cardiff thirty feet of sea wall called Winter Esplanade was washed away. Scores of houses were flooded, and the Sophia Gardens and Cardiff Arms Park became great Lakes.

Congresbury

Monday's storm was experienced in all its fury at Congresbury, where the lightning was very fierce and vivid, and the thunder deafening. A house near the Ship and Castle was struck by the Electric fluid, and practically split in two, a rent over a foot wide being made in the walls. Fortunately the occupants were not at home at the time. In another house and iron bedstead was wrecked, and the lightning is described as playing on the church tower 'like balls of fire'

End of Clevedon Mercury report .

Since 1899 we have suffered several minor breaches of the wall, but with modern machinery there has been no long period during which the tide has had its will and flooded the area without any check. One wonders however, what will the situation be in 50 years time? Are the pundits correct in their forecasting of an earth warming? Will the sea walls have to be built even higher? Or will the North Somerset moorland be left to nature as some people are already suggesting - to revert to salt-water marshes flooded twice a day at spring tides and just soggy mud flats on the neap ones.

Derek Lilly

❑ ❑ ❑ ❑ ❑

East Clevedon and its Old Farms

East Clevedon is the area around East Clevedon Triangle, including part of Old Street, Highdale Road, Walton Road and Tickenham Road. This part of Clevedon is believed to be the area from which the town got its name - the steep cleft between Strawberry Hill and Court Hill with the road passing through giving it the name Cleft-town. Because I will be dealing with farms and old industries in and around this area, I shall extend this history into the north eastern part of the old parish of Clevedon, including Norton's Wood Lane, Court Lane and Moor Lane.

Near the eastern boundary of the parish stands the ancient Manor house, Clevedon Court, parts of which date from 1320. The early known builder, John de Clevedon is believed to have built onto the remaining parts of the earlier house, which may have been used by Matthew de Moretania, the Lord of the Manor at the time of Domesday. The house, owned by the National Trust, having passed through many hands in the meantime, is the oldest inhabited house of its type in England.

Clevedon is a curious place; the Court and the oldest Church, St Andrew's, are two and a quarter miles apart. The Court is situated near easy access to Bristol both through Tickenham and Walton. The site of the Church is less easy to explain. For many years it has been thought that it was built at the western edge of the parish so that a beacon lit on the tower would act as a lighthouse to warn ships away from the rocks below. This was backed up by the mistaken idea that it had been built by the Augustine Canons of Bristol, who placed their Churches at the sea's edge to warn travellers away from a watery doom. But Clevedon's church, had already been standing at the edge of the cliffs for some 60 years when it was handed over to the Augustinians in 1257 with Portbury, Tickenham, Were and Poulett by the Diocese of Bath and Wells, 'saving the maintenance of vicars therein'.

Low-lying land needed to be drained for pasture and arable use in medieval times, because on the hills there was no water, unless artificial ponds were built. The hills are limestone which forms with many joints and cracks allowing water to run away rapidly. On the low-lying moorland, small fields were formed, the earth from drainage ditches was used to form banks, and hedges were planted atop the banks to stop the earth slipping back into the ditches.

Many of these small fields were concentrated along the length of Ken Road, where the land was less boggy. At East Clevedon there was access to the moors, held jointly by the Manors of Clevedon, Tickenham and Nailsea. The moor gate holder lived at East Clevedon. His job was to make certain that the right number of animals were being put on the moors, no more than Clevedon's entitlement, to avoid over-grazing. At this end of the Manor lay some of the great fields in which the Manorial farms were given strips of pasture ground; Clevedon Field below Tickenham, Houndsars, Hayworth and Manmoor.

Most travellers came through this end of the town, from Bristol, Portbury and Portishead to the north and the villages to the south- all making their way along the Walton Road. This was the best site for the Inn - the Old lnn. From Walton Road, some travellers would have gone into Tickenham, but many more would have been heading south, and gone along Old Street to turn left at the Triangle into Ken Road. The oldest smithy was on the Health Centre site in Old Street over three hundred years ago, where many of these travellers would have stopped for running repairs. As well as houses for the moor gate keeper and the blacksmith, there were farmhouses. There was a farm called Gaskins, taken over by John Carey in the early 1800s. The lane which led to this farm was called Carey's Lane, later to be renamed All Saints' Lane when the church was built.

At the other end of this lane stood Court Farm, This was built during the last years of the seventeenth century as the home farm to be used by the Steward of the Manorial Estate. The previous home of the Stewards had been Highdale Farm, which became derelict around this time. While Court farm was being built, Clevedon Court itself was let as a farmhouse, with some rooms reserved for the use of the Steward. The Elton family were the first Lords of the Manor for many years to use the Court as a dwelling house.

The Old lnn may have been the site of the farm owned by Nicholas Collett in the seventeenth century. Another of the Colletts, John Collett, whose grand-daughter Eliza Durbin married into the Elton family in 1776.

A farm of some considerable age was in the house which is now 136/8 Old Street, formerly Village Farm. This house was built in 1500, the oldest building in the town after the Court and St Andrew's Church (Highdale farm having been rebuilt). As well as being a farmer, the occupant had the task of looking after the gate to the Old Park, now Dial Hill. The Park was reached by means of a pathway which led along Highdale Road up through the woods into Old Park Road. The warren keeper himself lived in Old Park House, built later on within the Park itself. The Park was a remote and wild area, wild enough in 1670 to hide James Barber for three weeks! He had got a servant maid pregnant, taken property from his uncle and decamped into the Park out of the way of the Constable, whose aim was to make him pay for the keep of the child. He was caught, but escaped again by asking to change his clothes at a friend's house and leaving by the back door.

On the site of the old East Clevedon Hall on the corner of Meadow Road stood Meadow farm, leased in 1607 by Edwin Brock and Joan Bush. Meadow Road lies on an ancient footpath or 'footmere' which led to the moors and joined Moor Lane on the west side of the M5 roundabout.

Elver fishing was carried out in Old Street, from a farm which is now the sweetshop near the Health Centre. John Mulgrey took over the farm with the rights to the elver fishing in 1688; the previous farmer was Richard Newton, and the elver fishing was listed in the 1630 Survey of Clevedon. Foods were limited in those days, and the nutritious elver was a valuable addition to the table.

In the present Moor Lane lies Newhouse Farm, now the Craft Centre, rebuilt after a fire in 1630 by Sir John Knight. Around the corner in Court Lane, the heart of the present Clevedon Pottery was a house called Insoles dating from the seventeenth century. I shall mention the Pottery later on. As you enter Clevedon on the Tickenham Road, there is a large white farmhouse on the left, called East End Farm. In 1753, this was let to Edward Durbin and his son Henry. Henry was a chemist from Bristol, who later wrote of hauntings in the city, at the Lamb Inn near Lawford's Gate - an obscure literary connection! He gave one tenth of his income to the poor of Bristol for many years. When he took on the farm it was called Newhouse Farm, presumably having been rebuilt at some time by a previous tenant. It was leased in 1690 by James Ayres or Eyres, who had taken over from John and Joan Barnes, who rented it in 1662. Two cottages nearby date from the late 1700s, and on the opposite side of the road is another house belonging to the Hedges family during the 1800s, and possibly part of their estates at this end of the Manor.

Opposite the Court itself in the Tickenham Road were two houses which are now completely gone. One was a farm let to a Mr Boulton with a mere 2 acres to its name. In medieval times this may have been the home of the local fuller. The fulling of cloth was carried out in the Tucking Mills on the Land Yeo in the fields south of Clevedon Court. The water powered large wooden hammers set on eccentric cams. Workers moved the Bristol-woven woollen cloth around underneath these hammers to full, or felt it. The mills are documented in the 1630 Survey. They may have existed for many years before this date though, when John de Clevedon was the collector of the Wool Tax in 1342. Much of the weaving done by the trade guilds in Bristol would have been brought out to mills running on the clear waters of the Mendips to be fulled. At this time, Somerset was a greater producer of wool than the Cotswolds.

The other of these two houses was let to John Higgins, who managed the fish ponds in the field below to the south. These were filled from the river and and the fish stocked in them provided an important addition to the Manorial diet. Food was ever important, and the Lord of the Manor had the right to have his own mark cut into the beaks of the Clevedon swans.

Further smallholdings lay behind the Court itself on the edge of Court Woods. Queen Anne Cottage, just above the motorway, was lived in by John Williams in 1670, when he and his mother were accused of stealing a sheep. The next tenants were the Gaynards, who stole lead from the roof of St Andrew's Church and concealed it in a barn to be sold when the fuss had died down. Not exactly model tenants, either of them!

An even less ideal tenant was William Newbourne in 1612. He lived in one of the houses on Norton's Wood Lane, and had been expressly forbidden to take deer from the park there belonging to Lady Stalling. Foolishly, he thought no-one would hear his gun, but Stephen Myller and William Hayward of Walton heard the shot, saw the smoke and gave evidence against him. He was lifting the dead deer over the wall of Mr Wake's Park, now Court Wood, in order to hide it.

Another incident concerning deer took place on the moors, in a park of ground belonging to William Coles. The field is still called Deermead, and the deer was found dead in the Blind Yeo near Davis Lane.

After the Enclosure Act for Clevedon was passed in 1799, the moors in the eastern part of the Manor were enclosed and allocated to the farms in proportion to the amount of land already leased by the farmers. Many pieces of verge waste ground were sold off as building plots, and Old Street and the Walton Road gained many cottages at this time. A lot of the cottages in Old Street have been demolished, some new - ie dating from 1799 - some older. One of the older ones was Dale's Tenement, which was on the empty site between Avon Fabrics and the Salvation Army Hall. It was a satellite farm to Highdale Farm, let to John Dale in the seventeenth century. This may have been the farm to which the Old Barton belonged, now beneath the houses of Parnell Road.

Other farms were built on some of the old common field called 'Clevedon Field Near Tickenham' - Smeathyard to the east of the Roadway Lane, or Court Lane. The name Smeathyard, my uncle, Derek Lilly has found, is derived from a place where wildfowl were bred for shooting.

Norton's Wood is the name given to the north eastern part of Court Woods, which at one time belonged to the Norton family, of Abbot's Leigh. The lane into the woods links some houses of varied ages, some dating from the early 19th century and some very much older. From the Clevedon end going eastwards you will find the first few cottages on the right, which were built after 1820 by John Andrews. Two face the road, the third is at an angle to the lane, at the edge of the plot he bought from the Court Estate. In the woods south of this group of cottages stood the old lodge for the Little Warren, let to Richard Merrick in 1673. He had a set number of rabbits to maintain in the warren for the pleasure of the Lord of the Manor. The house is long gone, quarried away by the old Conygar Quarry. The name Conygar, of course, commemorates the existence of the warren, meaning that it was a gar, or enclosed place where rabbits, or conies were kept.

The house further along on the right is the Crate, named for the field behind it. This name signifies a small enclosure or croft, usually adjacent to a house. We may have here an example of assarting, or enclosing woodland, but there are not any leases surviving which date this croft. Opposite is another early nineteenth century cottage probably built by the Hedges family who held the land almost all the way to the far end of the lane in the late 1500s.

About a mile along there are more cottages built by the Hedges in the early 1800s. These are followed by the two really old house sites in the lane, Harley House on the left and East End Cottage on the right. Harley may be traced back to the occupation of George Stybbens in the late 1500s, followed in 1618 by Matthew, John and Edmonde Davis. The Hedges family follow, inevitably. East End Cottage was occupied by the Cottrell family in the 1630 Wake Survey, after which it became derelict in the hands of Francis Mulgrey to get the use of the land without paying house rent. It has since been rebuilt.

During the latter part of the seventeenth century, there was a national shortage of minerals. In Clevedon this meant that a licence was issued to breach the sea walls for the making of salt at Salthouse. A less well-known fact is that there were mining licences issued by the Earl of Bristol for lead to be mined on Court Hill and the Old Park on Dial Hill. The Earl mined on Court Hill himself, and the licence gave strict instructions about how near to the earl's diggings the other miners could dig. The mining was opencast - the grounds would have looked like the mines on Mendip at Charterhouse and Priddy, bumpy and unsightly. This was called gruffy ground, or groovy ground, and was to be filled in after mining finished. Here and there on the Old Park, the workings are left in the areas now called Bennett's Ripple and Rippleside Road. Most of the Court Hill has now gone under woodland, but if you fall into any ridged areas, you'll have the comfort of knowing they have been there for three centuries!

There have at times been various industries in East Clevedon - recently Hale's Cakes, Weech's Ladder Works and Percy Daniel's Organ Works. The Sunflower Pottery of Sir Edmund Elton is well-known and well-documented, so I will not expand on its history here, except to point out that its demise brought us the much loved Clevedon Pottery in Court Lane. William Fishley Holland came to Clevedon to help Sir Ambrose Elton with the pottery after his father's death. Due to changing fashions this was unsuccessful. He was allowed to set up his own pottery in the early 1920s, at first digging clay from the orchard of his cottage in Court Lane, then importing from Devon, where his roots lay in four previous generations of potters, the Fishleys of Fremington. In the 55 years of the existence of Clevedon Pottery some tens of thousands of pieces must been produced. The Pottery was on the itinerary of any self-respecting tourist of those days, too, advertised in all the local guide books as having reliable glazes and rich colouring. Holland had the sense to make commercially attractive as well as visually beautiful pieces. When I was a child, we each had a Clevedon Pottery mug for our cocoa at bedtime, and many Clevedon mantelpieces held fine examples of this local work. Holland had been offered a partnership by the great Bernard Leach before he came to Clevedon. Leach often visited here watching contentedly as Holland put handles on jugs and mugs.

This area of the town was the first to be consciously developed by the Eltons, as the Enclosures clarified the ownership of pieces of waste ground. The strips of ground along the steep slopes of Court Hill and Strawberry Hill were divided up into plots for those who needed houses, and Walton Lane and Carey's Lane, (All Saints' Lane), became gradually more populous. In fact, a house occupied by John Powell opposite Court Farm became the first licensed non-conformist meeting place in Clevedon in 1812. A bungalow now stands on the site. The 'first' which put East Clevedon ahead of the rest of the Village was the speculative building which was to follow close upon the cottages.

The Court Estate Agent was William Hollyman, a man of enormous ability and discernment, not one to miss a business opportunity. He purchased land at East Clevedon Triangle in 1823 and erected Ilex Cottage and Trellis Cottage. Part of Trellis Cottage became a shop very early on when a baker leased the house. These cottages were the first Regency houses in Clevedon, built with no specific occupant in mind, but with the idea that they would be attractive to people who wanted to set up small, select lodging houses here. William's next project was the building of

The Grove, on the site where the cooper's shop had been, opposite the Old Inn. On the south side of East Clevedon Triangle ten years later he built Rose Cottages, a pair of pretty, mock- Elizabethan cottages, one of which still has its original windows, with their delicate columns and drip-mouldings. He also built houses in Hill Road and Wellington Terrace, all to a very high standard and all very quickly leased out to interested incomers.

These changes resulted in deeper alteration to the lives of the local people than perhaps we have realised before. At the time of the first detailed Census in 1841, the main occupations were for men. They were engaged in farming, labouring, building, transport, running shops and making clothing or shoes. All the work of a self-sufficient village community. Forty years later, the same number of people were farming and labouring. An equal number of people had independent means. But in other fields there were dramatic changes. There was 50% growth in the number of people working in shops and making and selling clothes. Building workers had doubled, along with gardeners and servants. There were triple the numbers involved in trades connected with transport and travelling. But the biggest change was for women; there were no laundresses in 1841, and 23 in 1881. Women now worked as servants, where there had been no employment for them before.

Conditions were improving, slowly but surely, on many fronts. The Eltons were appalled at some of the living conditions endured in the cramped cottages and built Orchard Row as a model working terrace of four, three-bedroomed houses in the late 1850s. As soon as the tenants moved in, they decided to live in as few rooms as possible and get extra money from letting the space they did not use themselves - entirely defeating the object.

Sanitation was on its way, along with piped water, gas and last of all, electricity. The number of children was such that a Sunday School was set up when All Saints' was built in 1860, to become a day School in 1873. The increase of horse-drawn transport to and fro meant a new smithy, run by the Harris family in Walton Road for many years, and the delight of schoolchildren in the district. Transport further improved with the coming of the Portishead branch of the Weston, Clevedon and Portishead Light Railway in 1907. Hale's Cake Factory provided massive employment with its rapid expansion from a small bakery in Old Street. The factory had a wide distribution network after it was bought out by Lyons. On a visit to the West of Ireland we found that there was no local baker, and it was only possible to buy cakes that had travelled, like us, from Clevedon!

With the decision to promote Clevedon as a resort, the Elton family changed the life of the working man and created a life for the working woman. By the mid 1800s, employment in agriculture as the main occupation in East Clevedon had taken second place to the new opportunities offered by the incomers, who needed servants, laundry-workers and shopkeepers. A group of cottages round the pub had become a self-sufficient part of the growing town, with its school, its Church, its industries and its shops.

Jane Lilly

❑ ❑ ❑ ❑ ❑

Clevedon County Library

Clevedon's Free Library first opened its doors on Tuesday, 28th January, 1928, as a voluntary effort by two ladies with 100 books to lend. Now, 70 years later, there is a staff of 13 who spend time at Clevedon with around 26,000 books and audio tapes to lend and an integrated computer system helping to keep everything under control.

Subscription libraries and reading rooms had been a feature of Clevedon since the 1830's and by their nature were limited to those who could afford to use them. In the mid 1920's Mrs Margaret C. Sandford recognised what was felt to be a pressing need in the town for a free library available to all. She had, before her marriage, helped her mother Mrs Teulon in the running of the Clevedon Parish Lending Library so was familiar with the process and so together with Miss Muriel Thoms, they made enquiries for possible premises in which to operate a free library. Mr. R. D. Russell, a Stationer in Alexandra Road, next to the grounds of St. Peter's Church kindly agreed to allow the use of a fair sized room behind his shop. It was arranged that the Library should open three hours a week, an hour on Tuesday morning, in the afternoon on Thursdays and in the evening on Fridays.

One hundred books were obtained through the County Librarian, Colonel Stewart, whose headquarters were then at Burnham-on-Sea. On that first Tuesday morning 40 books went out. Then on Thursday afternoon a further 21 were borrowed so that there were only 19 books left for the Friday evening people.

More books had to be sent for and these arrived by train in wooden boxes each containing 50 books. After cataloguing they were put on the shelves and were soon taken out by members numbering over a hundred in the first week.

St John's School *Michael Horsfield*

The Library proved very popular and by the fourth year there were over 500 members and it wasn't uncommon for well over a hundred to attend in the hour.

More volunteer ladies had been recruited to assist in the running of the Library as the membership and stock of books kept on increasing. All the books were changed twice a year when they had to be listed, packed and returned to Burnham, this occurred at mid-year and also over the Christmas-New Year period when Mr. Russell needed his back room for his Christmas display. Everyone felt much indebted to Mr. Russell for the loan of his room which he continued to provide on a voluntary basis.

In the spring of 1932 the ladies felt that what they had started was going beyond the capacity of voluntary workers and a Committee was formed to bring to the notice of the Urban District Council the need for the Library to be taken over by the Council.

To this end a Public Meeting was arranged in April 1932, chaired by Mr. W. Fishley Holland of Holland's Pottery and with Col. Stewart, the County Librarian, as the main Speaker.

The Council then appointed its own Library Committee to confer with the Voluntary Library Committee and after some protracted negotiations over the next two years Mr. Russell was appointed as a salaried Librarian and the Council provided considerably extended shelving for the room in his shop for which he was paid a small rent. The stock was increased to some 2000 books and the library was enabled to be open during all normal shop hours.

The formal opening of the Library under the new arrangements took place on Wednesday 16th May 1934 in the presence of a number of Councillors, the County Librarian and some of the ladies who had voluntarily carried on the work for more than six years.

In 1935, the first full year of operation with longer opening hours, the number of books issued to borrowers was 44,704 being made up of 37,319 fiction, 4919 non-fiction and 2466 juvenile.

By 1942, the number of issues had risen to 63,150, falling off again to around 50,000 and staying at this level for about seven years until 1951/52 when it started to rise at a meteoric rate of about 6000 per year until in 1955/56 it was over 82,000 issues. All this was still in the back room of Mr. Russell's shop, it must have been bursting at the seams!

Way back in 1946 some effort had been made to find alternative premises but nothing positive transpired until 1954 when The Gentlemen's Club in Linden Road, which was then being used as a furniture repository, closed its doors and became vacant. After a further two years of negotiation and modification it was decided to transfer the library to the ground floor at Linden Road on September 1st 1956. At the same time a new Librarian Miss McSweeney was appointed and in her opening report paid tribute to all the hard work done by Mr Russell in his 20 years as Librarian and to his assistant Miss Norris.

The accommodation and fittings in the new library building were in a somewhat unfinished state and the County approved an amount to be spent on finishing, decorating and furnishing. All of this work went on while the Library was in service.

Another year passed before on Wed, 11th December 1957, at 3.00 p.m. the Linden Road Library was officially opened by County Alderman Mrs.E.M.Miller-Barstow M.B.E. M.P. to the applause of 100 invited guests.

A feature of the new premises was the provision of a proper Childrens Library in a separate room and during the opening ceremony Mrs Miller-Barstow visited this to meet some of Clevedon's younger readers. The adult section was now able to accommodate 6,500 books compared with the 4,000 in the old premises, with attention being given to a wider selection of reference books. In addition, the participation in the Inter-Library Loan System enabled readers to put in requests for books not in stock. Books came from as far afield as the Library of Congress, Washington, U.S.A and some one in the Armed Forces in Germany was lent,through the System, a book from Linden Road. In the Spring of 1958 Miss McSweeney left to take up another appointment and Mr. H.A.V. (Vic) Dawson was appointed as Clevedon's Librarian, a position he was to hold until his retirement in 1986.

For a number of years there had been 'rumblings' about there being no Library in the lower part of the town and the Council Library Committee debated the item a number of times and considered various possible locations. Finally, in May 1963, the ground floor of the former Midland Bank premises at 28, Old Church Road was leased and in December 1963 opened its doors as a Sub-Branch Library, but in the minds of the Library Committee it was very much an experiment as no other town in Somerset had two libraries!. It was going to be open all day on Wednesdays which, it was hoped, would develop into a new field of borrowing from people in shops and offices. The need for the Sub-Branch was soon confirmed because by the following September 25,246 books had been issued to members from a stock of 4,600 volumes.

Much to the dismay of the Librarians the upper floor at Linden Road had been leased out as a Civil Defence Headquarters and this continued until the Government abandoned the Civil Defence Scheme making it possible to take over this space and extend the library. Various modifications were necessary, not least the installation of a fire escape which meant the demolition of a very elegant wrought iron balcony. However by early 1971 all was complete, the extra space allowing a re-organisation of the non-fiction stock to make it freely available to borrowers and the provision of somewhere to sit and study.

Another feature of Clevedon's Library Service was the introduction of a Mobile Library operated from Linden Road to serve families who were not able to get to a branch library. The vehicle went into operation on 7th March 1959, carrying a selection of fiction, non-fiction and childrens books. Operation was based upon registration by families, not individuals, popularity being such that within four weeks over 5000 books had been issued to 1000 registered families. The service covered an area from Bristol to Weston-super-Mare and from a line through Dundry, Winford, Butcombe, and Puxton to the sea, but excluding areas which already had a branch library. There was no doubt that the mobile service was meeting a need because a review after the first seven months of operation revealed that 56,605 books had been issued to 1493 registered families. The Mobile Library, operated by Miss Clapp and her driver-assistant Mr. Heal, went out every week-day come rain or shine and only the severe winter of 1962-63 forced them off the road for nine days when first the doors froze shut and on trying to open them the electric wiring burned out, then the Calor Gas used to heat the vehicle froze up and finally, despite the anti-freeze in the engine it too froze up!

By 1972 the mobile service had grown to such an extent that it was decided to move its base to Nailsea, which, with its purpose built Library, was better able to cope with the administration of the service. Therefore, with a register of 2,543 families having been issued with 112,640 books during the year from a travelling stock of 8,260 volumes the Mobile Library was transferred to Nailsea on 30th September 1972. Clevedon Library was also responsible for the staffing and operation of two branches at Yatton and Congresbury, the stock shared between these sites and regularly circulated.

In April 1974,The County of Avon was created. In library terms this brought together the previously separate library services provided by Somerset County Council, Weston-super-Mare Borough Council, The City of Bristol, The City of Bath and Gloucester County Council creating the Avon Library Service.

The Linden Road and Triangle Branches continued to grow although a slow down, common to the rest of the Country, was noted in the returns for the 1972-73 period. Various theories were advanced including the spread of colour television, the mild winter, dissatisfaction with modern novels and increased affluence leading to more book buying rather than borrowing.

Whatever the reasons, the Staff at the Public Libraries continued to provide the readers of Clevedon with an up-to-date selection of books and augmented this with audio tapes, maps, jigsaw puzzles, pictures and microfiche. The growing library service together with the steadily increasing population of the town pointed to the need for a purpose built library building. The development of the southern part of the town looked to the Triangle area for shopping and services and the long, narrow ground floor Library sub-branch in Old Church Road was hard pressed to meet the needs of this burgeoning part of the town.

As long ago as 1977 it was accepted that it would be desireable to include a purpose built library in any development of the Triangle area. It wasn't until 3rd February 1993 that a Press Release from Avon announced that a new library for Clevedon would be opening soon in the former St. John's School in Old Church Road.

'Soon' was the operative word because on Monday 22nd February of that same year,1993,the doors of the new library opened for business! The Official Opening followed a few days later in March and the Opening Day photograph shows all the smiling faces expressing ,no doubt, the pleasure of having a new environment in which to work after all the years of less than ideal surroundings. This is the fourth life for this building which had started as a farm barn, became the fore-runner of St. John's Church, then when the new church was built and the

Staff and Officials at Clevedon Library Opening Day, March 1993

congregation moved over it became St.John's School and now it makes a very pleasant light and airy library with a most helpful staff under the leadership of the Librarian, Graham Tuckwell. April 1996 saw a further change in local government, and control of the library service, with the creation of the new unitary authority of North Somerset Council. This council now took on the role of the abolished Woodspring District and Avon County Councils so the library service was, once again, in local hands.

Just a few more statistics to bring the story up to date, the stock of books is around 26,000, plus 1,100 audio recordings, 120 jigsaw puzzles, 800 pictures, 150 maps and 1800 microfiche and in the 1996/97 year there were 209,476 issues made to approx: 12,000 members. On top of all this the North Area Library Manager Andy Brisley has recently been engaged in installing a new computerised book issuing system to link up N. Somerset's 12 libraries and 2 mobile libraries. It enables users to see what is in stock at any of these libraries and search for books. The system also provides a link up to libraries in South Gloucestershire, Somerset and Bath and N. E. Somerset providing users with a much wider range of books and other materials from which to choose.

This is a long way from the voluntary start 70 years ago with 100 books in the back room of Mr.Russell's shop, and we take off our hats to Mrs. Margaret Sandford, and her assistant Miss Muriel Thoms, for their far sighted effort to get the service adopted by the Council of the day enabling it to grow into what we have today.

Andy Brisley & Roy Girling

❑ ❑ ❑ ❑ ❑

ACKNOWLEDGEMENTS

This book could not have been compiled without the information readily given by so many people and in particular, thanks are given to:

Ms. J. Attwater
Mr. J. Bigwood
The Bristol Water Company
C.C.S. Local History Group Members
The Clevedon Mercury
Mrs. H. E. Dunn
Mr. C. Dyer
Mrs. M. Evans
Mrs. J. Fielding
Mr. & Mrs. R. F. Ford
Dr. R. Harrison
Mrs. Horsfield
Mr. C. Manners
Miss M. May
Mr. N. May
The Lancet
Mr. Lemar (Ex W.O.Royal Navy)
Mr. D. Parsons
Mr. C. A. Reading (Ex P.O. Royal Navy)
Mr. J. A. Roberts (Ex P.O. Royal Navy)
Rev. N. Sandford
Cllr. D. Shopland
S. Western Electricity Historical Society
Mr. J. Staddon
Mr. M. Stevens
Mr. C. Summerell
Dr. Tailby (Ex P.O. Royal Navy)
Mr. & Mrs. A. Willcocks
Dr. H. Wilkinson
Mrs. D. Woodman
Mr. R. Woolard
Mrs. P. Youde

❑ ❑ ❑ ❑ ❑